Homemade Halloween

Homemade Halloween

Fox
Chapel Publishing

1970 Broad Street • East Petersburg, PA 17520
www.FoxChapelPublishing.com

ISBN 978-1-56523-382-9

Models: Emily Cameron, Jesse Carmichael, Eric Cassini-Brochu, Linda Castle, Marie-Esther Chabot, Virgile Chabot, Gerard Dee, Colin Dion-Martel, Adrienne Fournier-Sirois, Julien P. Galarneau, Allison Home-Douglas, Ariel Home-Douglas, Chantal Kost, Philippe Kost, Madhuri Kumar, Anne-Marie Lemay, Nathaniel Lewis-George, Rob Lutes, Cecilia Melanson, Ashlinn Parsons, Brendan Parsons, Catherine Pigeon, Robert Ronald, Brittany Sigler, Lauren Sigler, Gregory Vadnais

Publisher's Cataloging-in-Publication Data

    Homemade Halloween. -- East Petersburg, PA : Fox Chapel
        Publishing, c2008.
        p. ; cm.
        ISBN: 978-1-56523-382-9
        First published in 2003 by St. Remy Media Inc. as "Celebrate
    Halloween."

    1. Halloween--Juvenile literature. 2. Halloween costumes--
    Patterns. 3. Halloween decorations--Patterns. 4. Halloween
    cookery--Juvenile literature. 5. [Halloween.] I. Title. II. Celebrate
    Halloween.

GT4965 .H66 2008
394.2646--dc22   2008

To learn more about the other great books from Fox Chapel Publishing, or to find a retailer near you, call toll free 800-457-9112 or visit us at www.FoxChapelPublishing.com.

Note to Authors: We are always looking for talented authors to write new books in our area of woodworking, design, and related crafts. Please send a brief letter describing your idea to Acquisition Editor, 1970 Broad Street, East Petersburg, PA 17520.

Printed in China
10 9 8 7 6 5 4 3 2 1

Homemade Halloween

TABLE OF CONTENTS

Let the Fun Begin!

This book is a treasure chest of ideas ranging from cool costumes to wear trick or treating to spooky special effects for a haunted house. Patterns and cutouts at the back of the book make easy-to-do projects even easier. Never made a lion's tail or a pair of angel wings? With photos and step-by-step instructions you'll learn what magic can be created with a piece of wire and a twist of the wrist. We'll show you how to carve a jack-o'-lantern and how to make a pumpkin come alive without carving. You want to give a Halloween party? Check out our selection of decorations, games, and recipes. Much of what you need to put together a spectacular Halloween may be found around the house. You can pick up the rest at your craft shop, hardware, or fabric store.

A Wealth of Material

The variety and types of material available in most fabric stores (or even at the back of your closet), are enough to give you ideas for all the Halloweens to come. Create from scratch or work in layers, adding on to existing 'foundation clothes'. Choose accesories carefully to add that all-important touch of magic or ghoulish detail.

Flexible, colorful and strong, pipe cleaners support as well as decorate.

Tricks of the trade: a traditional sewing kit with some 'hot' alternatives—a glue gun and Velcro™ adhesive strips.

Frightfully real, plastic and rubber creepy crawlers make that costume come alive!

The sturdy thickness of felt permits irregularly-cut shapes—a good choice for tunics, collars and hats.

Nothing puts the flash in a cape or regal robe like red satin. This 100 % acetate lining does the trick economically.

From the extra large to the delicate and petite, buttons, beads and decorative tunic hooks 'do up' costumes for princes and clowns.

Plush, printed fabrics with feline stripes and spots are just the thing for the wild at heart.

Sheer, light-weight and easy to shape, tulle is the ideal material for anything from a crinoline underdress to a ballerina's tutu.

Top of page: Radiatex, a polyester padding with a metallic-colored finish, is a sturdy and easy-to-cut covering for aspiring robots. Flashy fringe, spiralled two-tone cord, and a rainbow of ribbons and feathers make your Halloween palette unlimited.

5

Dandy Disguises

This chapter showcases an array of imaginative costumes, some made in minutes with cast-off garments, others that involve fabric, scissors, and a glue gun. Plunder closets and local thrift shops for special touches: a weathered fedora for a private eye, an eye patch and bandana for a pirate, and jazzy jewelry for a Roaring Twenties' beauty.

cutlass (page 26)

Our super sleuth completed his disguise with a magnifying glass, pencil, and a pad of paper. But where did he get that tie?!!

Hook (page 27)

Buckles (page 71) are fastened to a ribbon of elastic stapled in the back and slipped over black rubber boots.

For a rugged, ragged look, fringe the legs of an old pair of trousers.

Painting a spooky face on the sheet enhanced this ghost's disguise. The kerchief around her neck holds the eye and mouth holes in place so she can always breathe comfortably and see clearly.

Trick or treat carriers come in all shapes and sizes. For ideas on how to make your own, see pages 40-41.

Beads, a bandana, a paisley shirt, and—above all—a laid-back attitude are all this flower child needs to show she's hip. For tips on face painting see page 18.

This fabulous flapper has dressed to please herself. The dress was a lucky find, but any long-waisted dress will do, especially when set off by a feather boa and long beads. Her headband—a signature fillip for 1920 party girls—is decorated with a gaudy broach and a matching feather.

Don't forget to...

- **Check with the grown-ups before raiding their closets;** sometimes it's difficult to distinguish between a cast-off and a rarely used, but treasured, item.

- **Make sure you can see clearly and breathe comfortably—whatever the disguise.**

- **Keep small objects, like beads, balloons, and hard candy, from younger friends who might choke on them.**

- **Take care using long scarves, necklaces, and anything else that you wear around your neck.**

- **Adjust long dresses, oversized pants, and adult shoes so that you don't trip and hurt yourself.**

Capes & Cloaks

Face paint (page 18) instead of a mask was used here to make it easier to see when trick or treating.

This tunic, like Robin Hood's (page11), is made of felt. The side seams are glued together. The emblem "S," also felt, was glued to poster board before being attached to the front.

Superheroes, vampires, royalty, and magicians are just a few of the fabulous characters who depend on a cape or a cloak for authenticity. Fortunately they're easy to make; just cut and glue as we've shown here. Shop for remnants or use scraps of old fabric, choosing a material that hangs in soft folds.

1

2

The belt is a piece of fabric folded lengthwise, threaded through a felt buckle (pattern, page 71) and secured in the back with a safety pin.

Fold a large rectangular piece of fabric in half. (We used a 28"x 56" piece of red jersey for this superhero's cape.) For the neck, cut a quarter circle from one folded corner. Then cut a long connecting curve between the two opposite corners, as shown.

Cut a piece of ribbon about a yard in length and lay it along the collar. Fold a hem over the ribbon (make sure that the hem is wider than the width of the ribbon) and glue the edge down.

You'll Need

Materials for cape/cloak:	Tools:
-Fabric	-Scissors
-Ribbon	-Glue gun

You'll Need

Material for stand-up collar:
-Fabric (red and black)
-Wire hanger
-Electric tape

Tools:
-Pliers
-Scissors
-Glue gun

Count Dracula's face and hair (page 19) took less than a half hour to create.

The count's cloak is made in the same way as the superhero's (facing page)—but it is longer and has a stand-up collar.

1

2

For the count's collar, bend wire from a clothes hanger into the shape of a pentagon. Tape the wire ends together with electric tape. Wrap one side of the wire in red fabric and glue down the edges.

Cover the other side of the coat hanger in black fabric, leaving a couple of inches to overhang along the bottom. Bend the red side inward. Glue the overhang to the neck of the cloak, so that the black side faces out.

• Curving the count's collar around the back of the head will help keep it standing.

9

Terrific Tunics

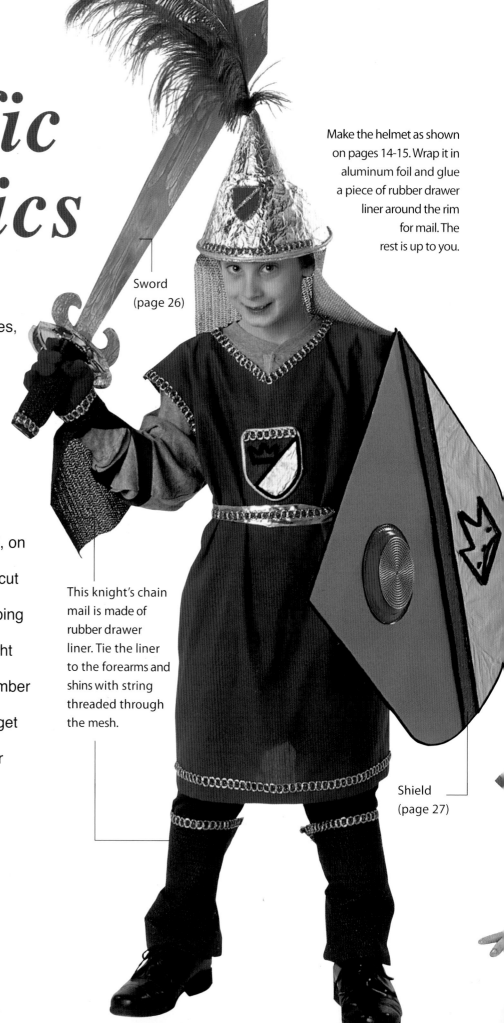

Gallant knights, medieval princes, archers, Native American princesses, and a slew of superheros don tunics when they dress for Halloween. Our knight is sporting a tunic made from a pillow case. Robin Hood, on the other hand, is wearing one cut from felt. Choose colors in keeping with the role—for example, bright colors for superheros, more somber ones for knights—and don't forget the hat (pages 14-15) and other accessories (pages 26-27).

Make the helmet as shown on pages 14-15. Wrap it in aluminum foil and glue a piece of rubber drawer liner around the rim for mail. The rest is up to you.

Sword
(page 26)

This knight's chain mail is made of rubber drawer liner. Tie the liner to the forearms and shins with string threaded through the mesh.

Shield
(page 27)

10

1

To make a tunic from a pillowcase, mark the openings for the arms and head with tape. Cut along the tape.

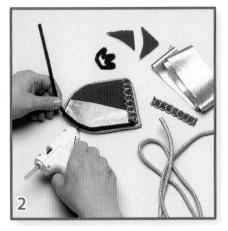

2

Every knight should bear an escutcheon or coat of arms on his tunic. We cut ours out of a royal blue pot scrubber in the shape of a shield, decorated it with gold and blue ribbons, and trimmed it with gold rope ribbon and black pipe cleaners.

You'll Need

Materials for knight's tunic:
- Large pillowcase
- Masking tape
- For the escutcheon; pot scrubber, ribbon, rope ribbon
- For the chain mail; rubber drawer liner
- String

Tools:
- Glue gun
- Scissors

Cap (page 15)

Quiver, bow, and arrows (page 26)

• Robin Hood's arrows are glued into the quiver to keep them from falling out.

A Tunic for Robin Hood

You'll need: green felt, suede ribbon, scissors, and a glue gun.

1. Cut a piece of forest green felt that is the width of Robin Hood's shoulders and twice the length between shoulders and knees.
2. Fold the fabric in half lengthwise and cut a hole in the middle of the fold for the head.
3. Cut a fringe at the shoulders and knees.
4. Make a fancy collar with triangles of light and dark green felt and suede ribbon—the same ribbon can be used as a belt.

Boxes & Boards

Sandwich boards and boxes form the basis of many fanciful costumes from Jack-in-the-box to the Queen of Hearts, from robots to dice. It all depends on your cunning choice of decorations. Our Pizza Girl comes all-dressed with a yummy variety of tasty tidbits made from felt, rubber, and paper cut in the shapes of mushrooms, pepperoni, green peppers, olives, and cheese.

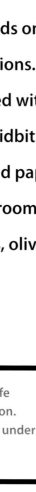

Make the chef's hat with scored white poster board rolled into a cylinder and secured with glue. Use white cotton stuffed with craft fill for the crown.

• Only use a craft knife under adult supervision.
• Only use a hot glue gun under adult supervision.

You'll Need

Materials for Pizza Girl Costume:
- Red foamcore
- Unbleached cotton
- Craft fill
- For pizza dressing, use scraps of fabric, bits of rubber, whatever strikes your fancy.

Tools:
- Craft knife
- Brown marker
- Glue gun

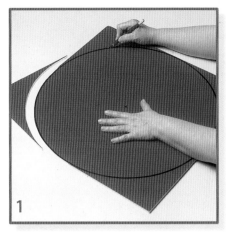

1

Outline the pizza shape on two pieces of foamcore. (We used 20"x20" pieces of red foamcore). Cut them out with a craft knife.

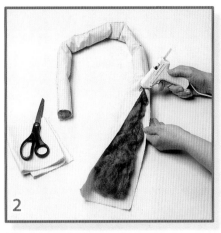

2

Wrap and glue long pieces of unbleached cotton around craft fill to make the crust. Glue the fabric rolls around the edge of the foamcore pieces and touch them up with brown marker or paint.

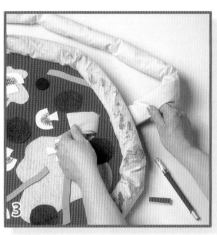

3

Now cut out shapes of your favorite toppings and glue them on. Make two more rolls of craft fill wrapped in cotton for the shoulder straps. Slip the ends through slits in the foamcore and glue the ends to the surface.

Face painting
(page 18)

A Box for a Robot

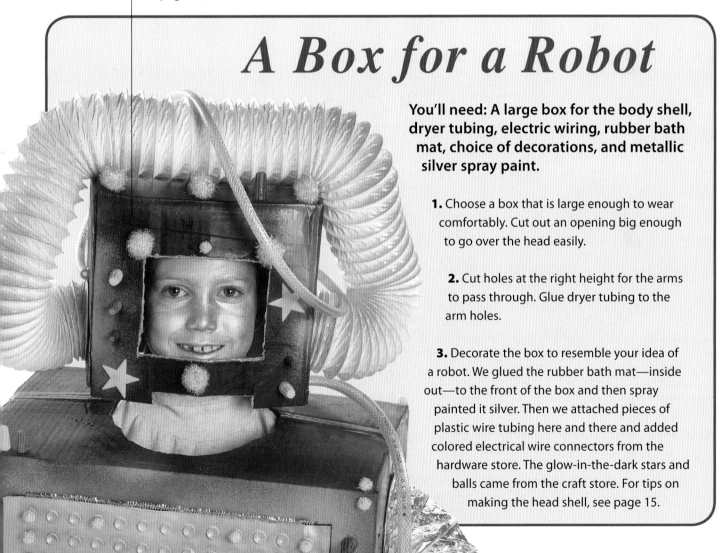

You'll need: A large box for the body shell, dryer tubing, electric wiring, rubber bath mat, choice of decorations, and metallic silver spray paint.

1. Choose a box that is large enough to wear comfortably. Cut out an opening big enough to go over the head easily.

2. Cut holes at the right height for the arms to pass through. Glue dryer tubing to the arm holes.

3. Decorate the box to resemble your idea of a robot. We glued the rubber bath mat—inside out—to the front of the box and then spray painted it silver. Then we attached pieces of plastic wire tubing here and there and added colored electrical wire connectors from the hardware store. The glow-in-the-dark stars and balls came from the craft store. For tips on making the head shell, see page 15.

13

Hatter's Heaven

The hat lies at the heart of most great disguises. Magicians and matadors sport cylinder hats. Witches and damsels—in distress and otherwise—are known for their cone-shaped hats. As for robots, the hat of choice is a box, cut and decorated with flair.

Create a festive witch's hat with orange rice paper and golden stars.

Trim the top and brim of a magician's top hat with black pipe cleaners and run a red or blue satin ribbon around the base of the crown. For an extra special touch add a pair of doves or a bunny from the craft store.

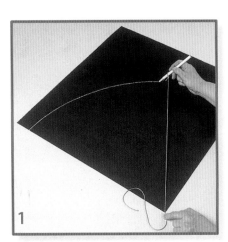

1

To make a cone hat, outline a quarter circle on poster board with string. (For a witch's hat use a 21" string.) Cut along the line. Roll into a cone and lightly tape the sides together. Adjust the hat to fit before securely gluing or taping the sides together.

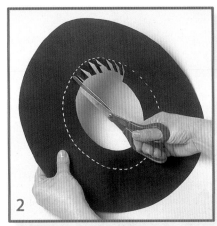

2

Stand the cone on another piece of board and trace around the cone. Draw a second circle 3" outside the first. Cut along this line. Draw a third circle 1" inside the first circle and cut along the line. Then cut slits to the first line to make a 1" fringe, as shown above.

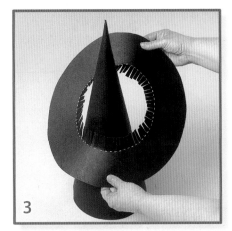

3

Slide the brim over the cone. Glue the fringe to the outside of the cone. Deco-rate it as you wish. Adding a band of wide ribbon will hide the glued fringe seam.

1

Make a medium-sized cylinder hat by rolling a rectangular piece of poster board (about 9"x 24") into a cylinder and gluing or taping the sides together. Roll it tighter if it is too big. Make a brim as described on facing page (step 2).

2

Cut a circle in poster board that has a diameter 2" longer than the diameter of the cylinder. Cut a 1" fringe around the circle and insert it into the top of the cylinder as shown. Glue the fringe to the inside of the cylinder.

Create a futuristic look with electrical supplies, silver metallic paint, dryer tubing, and antennae made of pipe cleaners and craft foam balls. Make sure the opening is large enough to see and breath comfortably

Consult patterns and instructions on page 72 for making Robin Hood's cap. Decorate it with suede ribbon and a feather.

To make the knight's helmet, follow the instructions on facing page (step 1) but use a 10" string instead.

You'll Need

Materials for Witch's Hat:
- Black poster board
- Orange rice paper
- Gold stars

Materials for Magician's Top Hat:
- Black poster board
- Ribbon
- Pipe cleaners
- Pair of doves

Tools:
- Pencil
- String
- Scissors/craft knife
- Tape
- Glue gun

Mask Parade

Wear a flashy mask to your next ghoulish gathering (pages 28-41) or turn mask-decorating into a party activity for your guests. Patterns for the masks shown here are at the back of the book. Cut them out and go to town decorating them with items found in a well-stocked craft box—paint, sequins, sparkles, pipe cleaners, felt, feathers, yarn, and craft foam balls.

You'll Need

Materials:
-Poster board
-Acrylic paint
-Sparkles and sequins
-Craft foam balls

Tools:
-Scissors
-Craft knife
-Paintbrush
-Glue gun

Trace the mask (pattern, page 74) on a sheet of poster board. Cut it out, using a craft knife to cut the openings for the eyes.

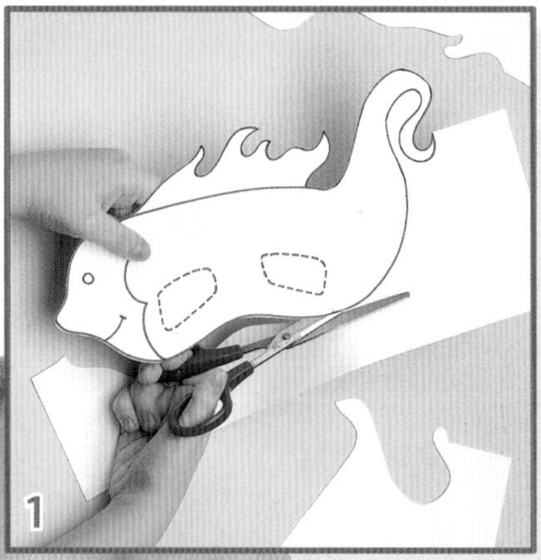

1

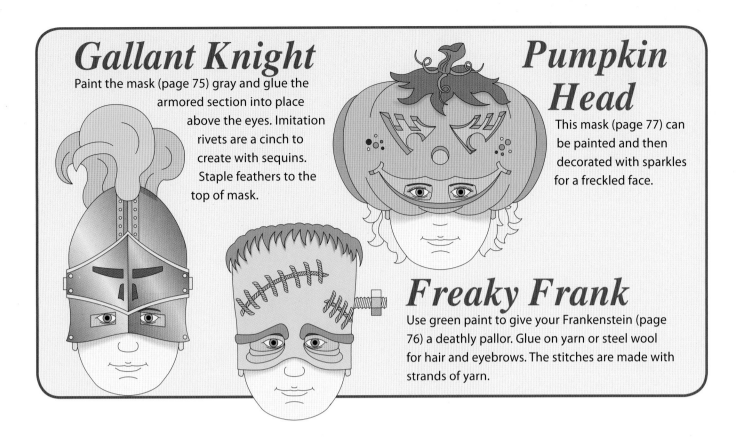

Gallant Knight

Paint the mask (page 75) gray and glue the armored section into place above the eyes. Imitation rivets are a cinch to create with sequins. Staple feathers to the top of mask.

Pumpkin Head

This mask (page 77) can be painted and then decorated with sparkles for a freckled face.

Freaky Frank

Use green paint to give your Frankenstein (page 76) a deathly pallor. Glue on yarn or steel wool for hair and eyebrows. The stitches are made with strands of yarn.

Decorate your fish with glittery scales made of sequins and sparkles. Pieces of felt cut into wavy shapes make great fins. Simply cut them out and glue them to the mask.

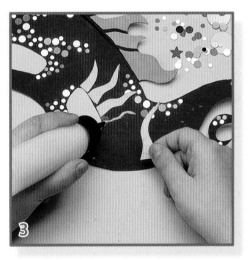

Paint the mask to your liking. Let each color dry thoroughly before applying the next one. You may want to experiment on a sample before beginning to work on the real mask.

• Make eye openings oversized so that you can see clearly.
• Don't wear masks to go out trick-or-treating.

Craft foam balls painted blue stand in as bubbles. Stick a pipe cleaner into each ball and tape them to the mask. Two more pipe cleaners secure the mask to the face.

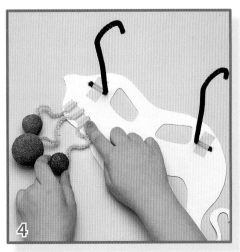

Face Magic

Makeup brings a world of fantastic characters to life. Use water-based cosmetics and check a theater supplier for special effects including crepe hair for a Bluebeard, tooth black for Captain Hook's front teeth, and glitter gel to brighten the face of your favorite Space Cadet.

• Only use cosmetics made exclusively for face painting.
• Test for allergies first by applying a dab to the inside of one wrist.
• Eyes should always be relaxed and closed when painting near them.
• Don't apply glitter gel or metallic powder near eyes.
• Don't use glitter or sequins on very young children.

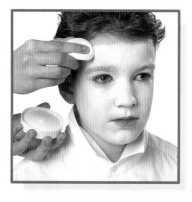

Whiteface is the base for clowns, vampires, ghouls, and grim reapers. Apply with a damp sponge using long strokes toward the center. One coat does it. A second only goes streaky. Let dry before adding colors.

Removing water-based cosmetics is easy. Just wipe the skin with a damp cloth. Then wash with soap and water.

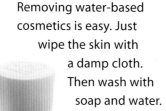

This little lion's telltale features are her nose and whiskers. Fill in the area above the upper lip and above the eyes with yellow. Using either a paint brush or cotton swabs, paint the whiskers, the nose, and the connecting lines in black. For the rest of her costume, see page 22.

Count Dracula's cloak, (page 9)

Count Dracula's ashen face is produced by applying a whiteface base. Darken the eyebrows and paint a widow's peak with black face paint. Spray paint the hair black with colored hair spray. Add the blood red lipstick, stick in some plastic fangs, and you're ready to go.

You'll Need

Materials:
- Whiteface performance makeup
- Water-based cosmetics
  - Selection of bright colored lipsticks
  - Glitter gel

Tools:
- Selection of different sized paintbrushes
- Cotton swabs
- Foam latex cosmetic sponges
- Soap
- Washcloth

Be as goofy as you like when it comes to clowns. Begin with whiteface, let it dry, then use bright colors to paint on exaggerated features. Arch the eyebrows, curl the lips, and don't forget the teardrops. For the rest of her costume, try outsize men's shoes (stuff the toes with paper so they fit), a white men's shirt, suspenders, and a bow tie—polka-dotted, of course!

... Face Magic

◀ Simple black and white lines combine to make a great spider-web face. After applying a layer of white, brush on seven thick black lines radiating outward from the tip of the nose. Use a smaller brush to create the thin black lines that form the webbing. The final touch—a plastic spider—can be glued on with spirit gum.

Fix face-painting mistakes by erasing only the part you want to change. Dab a moistened cotton swab on the area then dry with a fresh swab.

This clown face relies on facial features and painted outlines to accentuate colors and shapes. First, ring the blue triangles and yellow star with a contrasting orange line. Paint the nose by following its curves with red, and align the ends of the extended mouth with the outside corners of the eyes. The final touch—a rainbow wig—gives all your colors a knockout ▶ punch!

Toddlers without the patience for an extended makeup session will appreciate this quick and easy rabbit face. First, sponge on a light gray wash above the upper lip to create a realistic background for whiskers. Brush the whiskers on by adding black dots and three or four lines on either side. Outline the two rabbit teeth in black below the lower lip, then fill them in with white. Furry fabric ears and a pink triangle nose add final bunny touches.

Just like a real butterfly, this beautiful winged creature begins with a caterpillar body. Start by drawing a black outline of a circle for the head, then add the long body down the center of the nose. Fill in the shape, then add white lines to give it dimension. Test your artistic flair by adding the symmetrical spiral antennae, beginning with thick lines, trailing off to thinner ones. Outline the upper wings in orange, the lower ones in purple, then fill in the shapes with lighter colors applied with a sponge. Add the wing spots after the base colors have dried. For an added iridescent

Blend colors together by working in layers. Sponge on the first color. Let it dry. Then with an almost dry sponge, add a deeper or lighter tone, allowing the first color to remain visible.

◀ Show a sensitive side to Halloween with this sad Pierrot. The white bathing cap not only keeps hair clear of the face paint, but lets the eyes, mouth, and stark coloring stand out. Paint on short blue-black rays to accentuate the eyes. Extend the center portion of the mouth in red to create a pouting expression. Finally, apply the single large tear in deep blue, then highlight it in a lighter tone.

To find just the right ghoulish tone for Frankenstein skin, experiment with mixtures of green, yellow, and blue. Cover the face and ears by sponging on the chosen mixture. Deepen eye sockets with dark blue or purple. Brush on the head scar and lips in a deep ochre, then add creases and cracks in dried-blood red. For some extra-gory detail, add more dripping blood to the ▶ corner of the mouth. Heavy black eyebrows, applied with a thick brush, increase the visual weight of the head, which is crowned with a mop of gelled hair.

Heads & Tails

Ears and a tail—ably assisted by dramatic makeup (page 18)—are all that are needed to carry out the magical transformation from human to beast. We went a step further with this lovely lion, dressing her for a cool Halloween evening in a body suit made out of thick fleece—cut to her shape and glued along the seams. But a sweat suit would have sufficed.

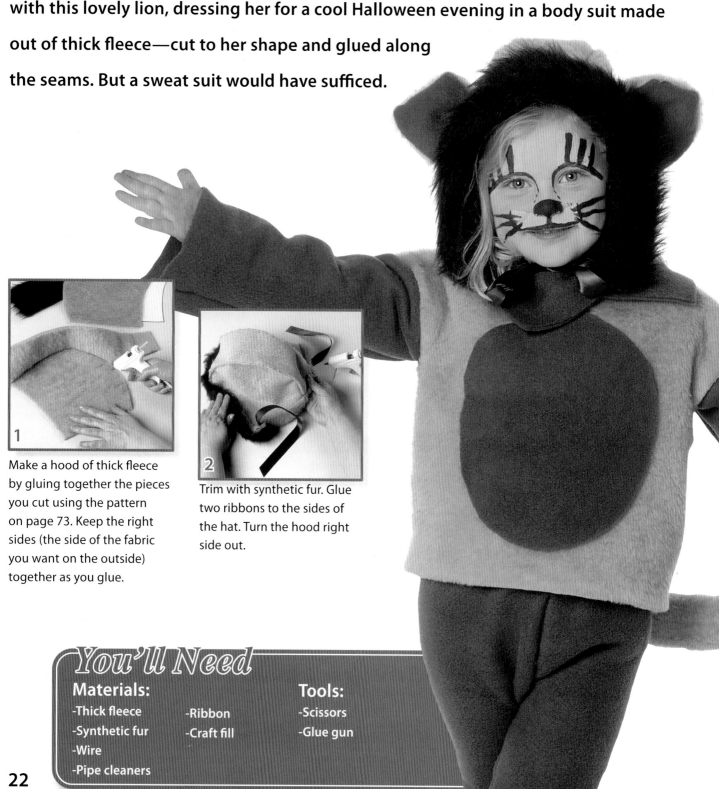

Make a hood of thick fleece by gluing together the pieces you cut using the pattern on page 73. Keep the right sides (the side of the fabric you want on the outside) together as you glue.

Trim with synthetic fur. Glue two ribbons to the sides of the hat. Turn the hood right side out.

You'll Need

Materials:
- Thick fleece
- Synthetic fur
- Wire
- Pipe cleaners
- Ribbon
- Craft fill

Tools:
- Scissors
- Glue gun

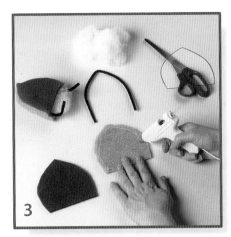

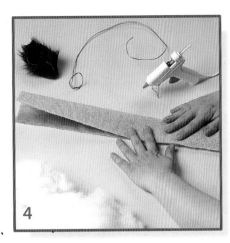

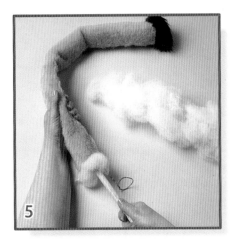

For ears, cut four fleece pieces using the lion ear pattern on page 73. Glue two pieces, right sides together, and let dry. Repeat for the second ear. Turn the ears right side out. Bend two pipe cleaners into U-shapes and insert them into the pockets for shape. Fill with craft fill and glue to the hood.

For a long tail, cut out a piece of fabric at least 6" wide. Fold in half lengthwise, right sides together, and glue to form a tube. Turn the tube right side out.

Glue a piece of synthetic fur to one end. Insert a piece of wire the length of the tail. It should be bent at one end and looped at the other. Stuff the tail with craft fill. Seal it closed and glue it to the back of the costume.

• One way to attach a tail is to cut a hole in a piece of fabric, pull one end of the tail through and glue it on the inside. Then secure the fabric to the seat of your pants with safety pins.

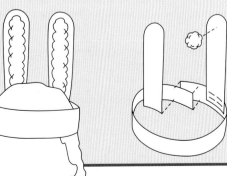

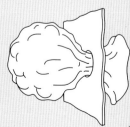

Devil

Poster board horns protrude through slits in the top layer of a fabric headband stiffened with wire. For the tail, stuff a long red or black stocking and glue a triangle of felt to one end. Cut out a pitchfork (also poster board) and wrap it in aluminum foil.

Rabbit

Make ears and headband from poster board and a fluffy tail with cotton wool and fabric. Draw big bunny teeth and whiskers on your face. Don't forget to carry a carrot!

Winged Wonders

The paper wings for this divine creature are made with wire and natural fiber wrapping paper. Modify the shape of the wings and use different kinds of fabric and paper and you'll come up with any number of winged wonders. Then make the wings your very own by your personal choice of decorations.

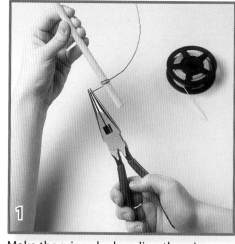

Make the wings by bending the wire into the shape you desire. (We used two pieces of wire to create a heart shape for the princess.) Wrap the wire ends around the wooden dowel.

Our cone hat (page 14) is wrapped in gold fabric and trimmed with a garland of gold stars

Magic wand (page 27)

We found this white cotton cassock—once worn, no doubt, by a young chorister—in our local thrift shop. If you have no such luck, use a white sheet or a length of white fabric. Cut a hole for the head, trim the length, and glue gold trim around the edges.

You'll Need

Materials:
- Natural fiber wrapping paper
- Wire (18 gauge)
- Wooden dowel
- Garland of stars
- Elastic tape

Tools:
- Pliers
- Glue gun

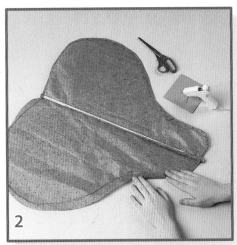

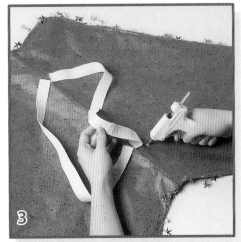

Cover the wire frame in wrapping paper (or material) and secure with glue or tape. Flip the wings over and repeat wrap the other side. We glued on a star garland.

Cut strips of elastic tape for shoulder straps and glue their ends to the wooden spine. Now you're ready for flight.

• Be careful when working with wire pieces; their ends can poke and scratch.

Butterfly
Stretch brightly colored cellophane over the wings and then decorate with cutouts of cellophane in contrasting colors. Paint your face (page 18).

Bird
Wrap the wire frame with a light fabric and glue on an array of feathers. For the beak, consider a mask cut out of poster board and decorated with more feathers.

Bat
Black tulle or other gauzy fabric would create the effect of bat wings. Use the method shown on page 23 to make bat ears and wear a black leotard and stockings.

Dragonfly
Transparent cellophane suggests the delicacy needed for dragonfly wings. For antennae, stick craft foam balls to the ends of two pieces of wire, which are wrapped around a headband.

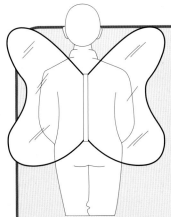

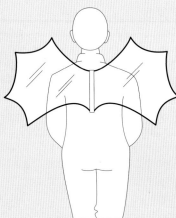

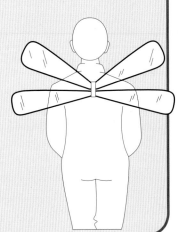

Tools of the Trade

Basket

Grip

Basket

What's a pirate without a hook, a knight without a sword, or a fairy without a magic wand? The right accessory can transform a collection of old clothes into a convincing costume. Don't forget your local thrift store. While you're not likely to find a magic wand there, you might discover a battered violin case, long satin gloves, a butterfly net, some truly outstanding pieces of costume jewelry, the absolutely perfect set of opera glasses. . .

Cutlass
Cut the blade from foamcore and the basket and grip from craft foam sheets (patterns, page 70). Spray paint the blade silver. Cut slits in the basket and slide it on the blade. Glue extra bits of foam sheet to both sides of the basket to help keep its shape.

Latex arrow head

Bow, Arrow, and a Full Quiver
Notches for holding the string secure are the key to a great bow. For the rest of Robin Hood's attire see page 11.

Sword
Foamcore makes a perfect sword (pattern, page 70.) Paint it silver and use an aluminum plate for the basket. For the rest of the knight's garb see page 10.

The quiver was made out of a poster tube wrapped in a thin layer of cork. The arrows ar e wood dowels topped with feathers from a duster and secured to the inside of the quiver with glue.

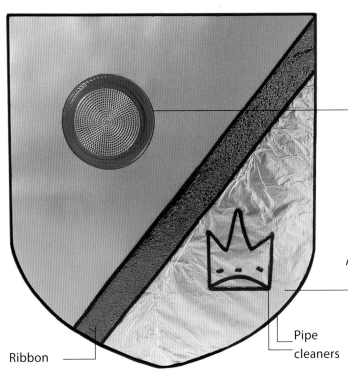

Shield

We cut a 20"x24" piece of foamcore into the shape of a shield. The handles (hidden in back) are made with elastic tape like those for the wing's shoulder straps (page 25, step 3).

Blue plastic plate with a plastic canvas for embroidery glued to the bottom.

Aluminum foil

Pipe cleaners

Ribbon

Magic Wand

We made the star with a piece of wire. After gluing paper to the wire and gluing the wire to the end of a wooden dowel, we painted the whole thing gold and added a trim of gold pipe cleaners. For the rest of the divine costume see page 24.

Hook Hand

The hook is a plastic clothes hanger passed through a hole cut in the bottom of a yogurt container wrapped in aluminum foil. If you use a wire hanger, make sure you wrap the ends in electric tape. For the rest of the pirate costume see page 6.

Starstruck Clown

All this clown needed to get in the mood was an oversized bow tie, makeup, and an arrow through his head. We used craft foam for the head and for the fletching. the arrow, cut a wooden half, twist the ends of a of wire around the free the two rods, and bend curve over the shape of the cushioning, slip on a couple of foam rings or latex washers.

Ghoulish Gatherings

Create a magical atmosphere where wizards, witches, and warlocks will feel right at home. Stencil a tablecloth with glittering stars and moons and build a haunted castle to reign over the party table. Read on for ideas on how to entertain your friends with games (pages 30-35) and tasty Halloween party fare (pages 36-41).

You'll Need

Materials:
- Tablecloth
- Poster board
- Acrylic paint
- Glitter fabric paint

Tools:
- Craft knife
- Fine paintbrush

1. Using a craft knife and a cutting mat, cut poster board stencils (patterns, page 71) of stars and crescent moons.

2. Stencil the tablecloth with gold acrylic paint. Use a fine paintbrush and stroke inward toward the center of the stencil.

3. Once the paint has dried, apply glitter fabric paint to the edges of the stars and moons.

- Craft knives are very sharp. Only use them under adult supervision.
- If you don't have a cutting mat to cut on, use a piece of heavy cardboard instead.

This castle is made with two differently shaped cardboard boxes, glued to one another and roofed with corrugated cardboard. The drawbridge is a perforated metal plate picked up at the hardware store and hung with wire.

The towers and chimneys are cardboard tubes from gift wrap or toilet paper, trimmed with crenellated corrugated cardboard.

The wizard's hat (page 14) and cloak (page 8) are decorated with stars, planets, and crescent moons (patterns, page 71).

The ribbon pennants are held aloft by 18 gauge wire.

The beard was cut from white synthetic fur from the craft store. Cotton wool would have worked as well.

Fun & Games

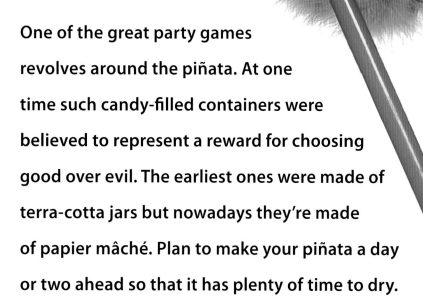

One of the great party games revolves around the piñata. At one time such candy-filled containers were believed to represent a reward for choosing good over evil. The earliest ones were made of terra-cotta jars but nowadays they're made of papier mâché. Plan to make your piñata a day or two ahead so that it has plenty of time to dry.

- Make sure you cut a trapdoor large enough to fit the treats.
- Try using the kind of balloon used for helium—it will stand up to the pressure of being covered by papier mâché better than a regular party balloon.

Playing Piñata

- Hang the piñata in the center of the room. Clear away furniture, lamps, and bric-a-brac from the surrounding area.
- Let the children have turns being blindfolded and taking a whack at the piñata with a broom handle. Sooner or later the piñata will break spilling the candy and toys on the floor.
- While each child is taking a turn, keep all the other children at a distance to avoid any accidents.

Blow up a balloon and knot the end. Dip strips of newsprint into wallpaper paste and lay them on the balloon in all directions, brushing on a thin coat of glue as you go. Let the first layer dry. Apply a second layer, and for an extra-strong piñata, add a third layer the same way. Let the piñata dry for at least 24 hours before continuing.

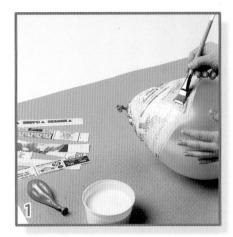

When the papier mâché has dried, tape a loop of string to the end of the piñata for hanging. Cut open a trap door at the other end (the balloon will pop) using a craft knife. Fill the piñata with wrapped candies and small toys. Close the trap door and cover it and the tape holding the string with a layer of papier mâché.

Before painting your design on the piñata, apply an undercoat of white paint. For our spider, we painted colorful stripes and then filled in with black paint.

For the spider's 8 feathery legs, wrap different-colored boas around pieces of wire and glue their ends to the wire tips. Bend the wires and glue or tape the ends to the piñata. We glued on candy, bits of paper, and googly eyes from the craft store to make the spider's funny face.

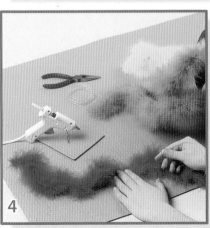

You'll Need

Materials:
- Balloon
- Strips of newsprint
- Wallpaper paste
- String
- Masking tape
- Acrylic paint
- Feather boas
- Wire (18 gauge)

Tools:
- Paint brushes for paste and for paint
- Craft knife
- Glue gun

31

More Fun &Games

Who am I ?

- Inscribe the names of roles, such as the Wicked Witch of the North, Dr. Frankenstein, Count Dracula on paper headbands.
- Distribute the headbands among your guests without letting them see what is written on their own handband.
- Encourage your guests to question one another about the identity of the character they are wearing.
- All questions are permitted EXCEPT "Who am I?"
- The ONLY permitted response is either "yes" or "no."

Bobbing for Apples

- Fill a wash basin with water and set it on newspaper or towels.
- Drop in some fresh apples.
- Let your guests take turns trying to grab an apple with their teeth. They must keep their hands behind their backs at all times.

Warning: This is a hilarious game with lots of spill over. Keep plenty of towels nearby to mop up!

A Haunting Tour de Farce

Design a horror-filled tour that your guests will never forget! Set a table with bowls filled with various cold food items designed to represent body parts. For example:
• Cold cooked spaghetti for vampire entrails; • Peeled grapes or lichees for cat's eyes; • Gelatin for witch's guts; • Cold cooked oatmeal for human brains.

Blindfold your guests one at a time and lead them into the dimly lit room and let them touch the food. As they sink their hands into each bowl, you explain in the spookiest tones you can muster what part of the human body they are touching! To enhance this ghoulish experience, hang fake cobwebs (available from craft stores) and play a recording of eerie music such as classical music in a minor key, organ music, the music from the Phantom of the Opera, or Thriller by Michael Jackson.

Terror Theater

Create a scary pantomime in silhouette. Encourage your guests to make up stories around their Halloween costumes. Then set the stage by hanging a bed sheet from a clothes line strung across the room or supported by pieces of furniture. Place a light about five feet behind the sheet. Turn out all the other lights and invite everyone to take a turn acting out their stories.

A Touch of Magic

No Halloween party is complete without a little supernatural wizardry. Here are three baffling secrets of illusion passed down from some of the greatest magicians of all time. With a little practice and the few simple props shown, you can defy the rules of science and probability, and entertain and amaze your friends, too!

The unbreakable cord

1 Hold an 18-inch length of cord in one hand, looped under your thumb. Hold a second, short loop of cord so the loop sticks up above the edge of your hand.

2 Without letting your audience see the palm of your hand, have a volunteer cut the second loop of cord with scissors.

3 Now pull the dangling ends of the first cord, making sure to grab hold of the cut pieces in one hand. The cord mysteriously remains uncut.

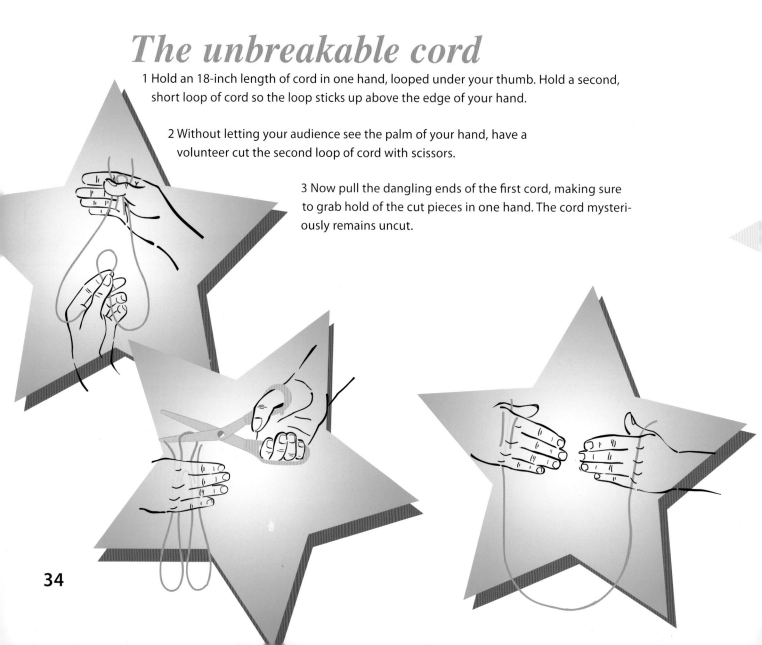

34

The floating wand

• Grab your wrist with the opposite hand, holding a Popsicle™ stick across your palm. Now, with your free hand, pick up the magic wand and slip it under the stick.

• Make sure that your audience sees only the back of your free hand, and that all your fingers are visible. The magic wand appears to float in midair.

Card chaser

1 Shuffle the cards, then just before setting the deck face down, make sure that you see the bottom card. This is the "key" card for the trick. Remember it!

2 Have a volunteer pick a card from the deck and look at it without showing it to you. Have him or her place the card on the top of the deck.

3 Now have your volunteer cut the deck. Your "key" card is now somewhere in the middle.

4 Fan out the cards, and pick out the card immediately to the right of your "key" card and show it to your volunteer. This is their chosen card!

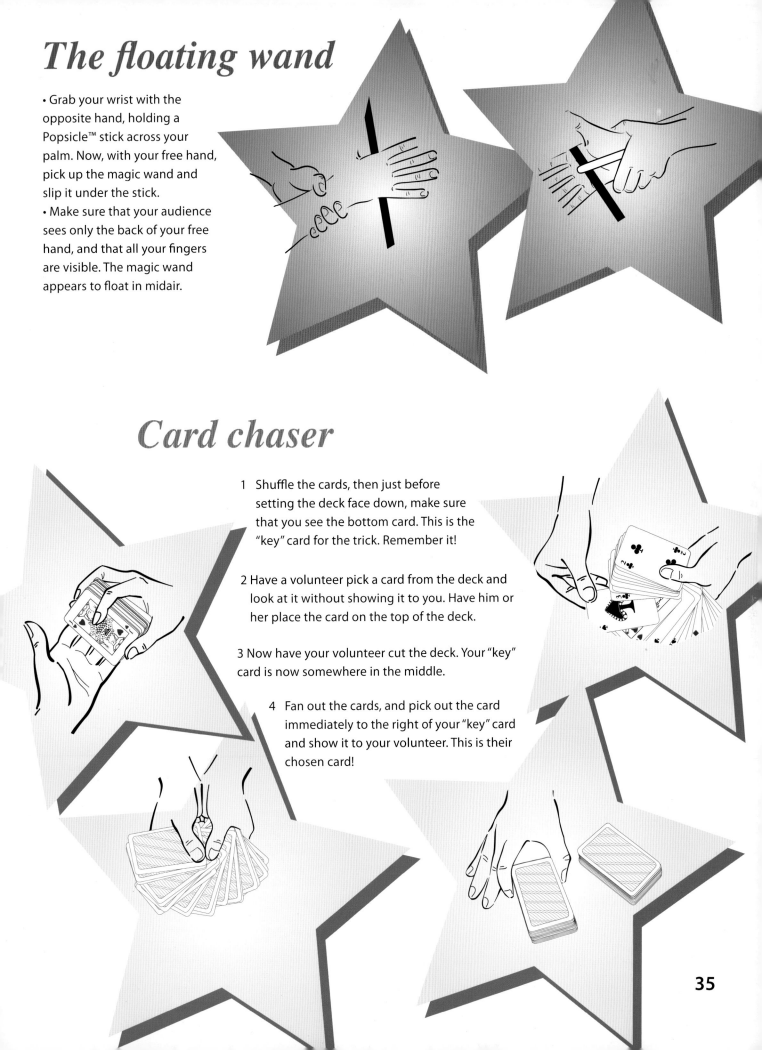

Party Fare

Here's a selection of yummy recipes to tempt your guests. Serve some nutritious food to start, but keep it simple. Consider a pumpkin soup accompanied by crackers and cheese or perhaps hamburgers served with garden fresh vegetables and a variety of store-bought creamy dips. Then you can lay out the cakes, cookies, cupcakes, and, of course, candy. Make the food preparation a family affair—decorating the food especially can involve all ages.

Delicious Pumpkin Soup

(Makes 8 servings)

3 cups pumpkin cut into 1/2 inch cubes

1 cup water

1/2 teaspoon salt

4 cups milk

1 egg

3 tablespoons flour

Pinch of salt

Pinch of ground cinnamon

Sugar to taste

- Put pumpkin, water, and salt into a soup pot. Bring to a boil.
- Reduce heat and simmer for about for 5 minutes or until pumpkin is easily pierced with a fork.
- Mash pumpkin with a potato masher (or use a food processor).
- Bring milk to a boil and add it to the pumpkin, stirring as you pour to remove any lumps.
- In a separate bowl, beat the egg. Add the flour and a pinch of salt. Whisk together until smooth.
- Slowly add egg and flour mixture to the pumpkin, whisking again to keep soup smooth. Reheat, but don't boil.
- Flavor with a pinch of cinnamon. Add sugar to taste.

- Read the recipe carefully before you start and make sure you have all the ingredients you need.

Veggie Platter and Dip

Choice of green, red, and orange vegetables such as celery, sweet peppers, carrots, cucumber, and tomatoes
Selection of ready-made creamy dips

- Wash and cut the vegetables for eating.
- Arrange the vegetables around portions of dips on a large platter.

Eye-of-Bat Fruit Salad

Choice of orange and yellow fruit such as oranges, pineapples, and cantaloupes
Purple grapes

- Peel and segment oranges and cut pineapple in chunks. Scoop cantaloupe into balls. Wash grapes.
- Serve fruit in large bowl or hollowed out pumpkin. Chill and serve.

Citrus Punch

1 12-ounce can of frozen orange juice concentrate

1 12-ounce bottle of white grape juice

60 ounces ginger ale

1 pint lime sherbet

Green food coloring

- Mix together all the ingredients and add two or three drops of green food coloring.
- Chill and serve in a punch bowl with slices of lime and orange floating on top.

Witches' Brew

2 quarts sweet apple cider

1 12-ounce can of frozen orange juice concentrate

3 cups water

1/4 cup lemon juice

1 teaspoon ground ginger

Cinnamon sticks

- Put all ingredients into a soup pot and mix. Bring to a boil. Reduce heat immediately and simmer for 5 minutes.
- Carefully pour into a large punch bowl. Ladle into mugs. Garnish with cinnamon sticks.
- Delicious served chilled as well.

Party Fare

Creepy Cupcakes

(Makes 2 dozen cupcakes)

1 32-ounce package vanilla or chocolate cupcake mix

1 16-ounce container ready-made vanilla icing

Orange and black food coloring

Candy for decorating, such as miniature marshmallows, jelly beans, jelly worms, licorice candy, candy-covered chocolate

For chocolate hats: 1 box semisweet baking chocolate, 1 teaspoon shortening, miniature ice-cream cones, cookie wafers

- Preheat oven to 350°F.
- Make cupcakes according to instructions on package. Pour into cupcake mold and bake until a fork inserted into the center comes out clean.
- Divide icing into two separate bowls. Mix orange food coloring in one and black food coloring in the other. Spread icing on the cupcakes and decorate with candies.
- To make chocolate hats, melt baking chocolate and shortening in a double boiler. Dip cones and wafers into chocolate. Set cones on top of wafers and place on a plate covered with wax paper. Chill until chocolate has hardened.

Sweet Rice Balls

(Makes 1 dozen rice balls)

1/4 cup butter

40 marshmallows

1/2 teaspoon vanilla

6 cups puffed rice cereal

Candy for decorating

White corn syrup

- In a large saucepan, melt butter over low heat.
- Add marshmallows and stir until melted. Remove from heat.
- Add vanilla and puffed rice cereal and stir until well blended.
- While the mix is still warm, shape 1/2-cup servings into balls. Decorate with candy. If necessary, dab candy in corn syrup first to help stick.

Chocolate Pumpkins & Ghosts

(Makes 2 dozen cookies)

1 dozen vanilla-filled chocolate wafers

1 dozen gingerbread men (break the legs off to make them look like ghosts)

2 boxes white baking chocolate

Orange food coloring

Black candy for decorating, such as licorice jelly beans

White corn syrup

- In a double boiler, slowly melt white chocolate
- Dip the gingerbread cookies in the white chocolate and lay on wire rack to cool.
- Add orange food coloring to remainder of white chocolate.
- Dip chocolate cookies in the melted orange-colored chocolate and lay on wire rack.
- Before cookies cool decorate with candy. If necessary dip candy in corn syrup first to help stick.

38

Tricolored
Ice Cream Dessert

Orange, licorice, and vanilla ice cream

1 banana per serving

Candy for decorating

Chocolate syrup

- Place one scoop of each kind of ice cream in a bowl.
- Decorate with sliced banana, candy, and chocolate syrup. Serve immediately.

Sherbet Wizards

1 large orange per serving

Orange or lime sherbet

1 miniature ice cream cone per serving

Candy for decorating, such as sprinkles, candy-coated chocolate, jelly beans

- Using a sharp knife, cut off the top quarter of the orange and cut out the fruit.
- Fill orange peel with sherbet.
- Top with a miniature cone dipped in chocolate (see recipe for Creepy Cupcakes).
- Decorate with candies and store in freezer until ready to serve.

Caramel
Apples

(makes 6 candied apples)

6 apples, preferably McIntosh

1 large package of caramels

2 1/2 tablespoons water

6 popsicle sticks

Greased wax paper

- Wash and dry apples.
- Insert popsicle sticks into the stem end of each apple.
- In a medium saucepan, melt caramels with water over low heat. Stir occasionally.
- Dip apples into melted caramel and set to harden on wax paper.
- Chill until ready to serve.

Party Fare

Halloween Cake

2 32-ounce packages vanilla or chocolate cake mix
2 16-ounce containers ready-made vanilla icing
Orange and green food coloring

- Preheat oven to 350°F.
- Mix two cake mixes according to the instructions on the package and pour into two round stainless steel cookware bowls (9" diameter at top, 4" deep).
- Bake the cakes for about an hour until a toothpick inserted into their centers comes out clean.
- Cool on a rack. Remove cakes from cookware.
- In a small bowl, mix green food coloring with a small amount of icing.
- In a large bowl, mix orange food coloring and the remainder of icing.
  - Slice a 1" layer from the flat side of each cake to be used later for the pumpkin's stem.
- Fit the cakes together so they form a globe, spreading a thin layer of orange icing in between.
- Cover the entire globe with the rest of the orange icing.
- Shape a stem on top of the cake using the bits of cake cut earlier and green icing. If necessary, use toothpicks to support the shape and attach the stem.
- If desired, decorate with licorice rope to suggest the ridges of a pumpkin.

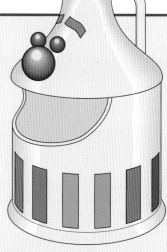

Totes for Treats

Design your own containers to tote your candy when you go trick-or-treating. Decorate one to match your disguise or make a thoroughly original one that goes with nothing at all. Here are some ideas to get you started:

A bird in the hand (filled with candy of course) is definitely worth two in the bush. For this bird you'll need: a cardboard box, scissors, glue, acrylic paint.

If this **candy monster's** greed gets out of hand, hang it by a belt over your shoulder. To make it you'll need: a clean plastic container (for bleach or fabric softener), poster board, marbles, a ping pong ball, colored markers, scissors, glue gun.

Treasure Island Cake

2 32-ounce packages of vanilla or chocolate cake mix

2 16-ounce containers of ready-made vanilla icing

Blue and green food coloring

Almond paste

Candies for decorating, such as jelly worms, jelly beans, chocolate coins wrapped in gold foil

White corn syrup

- Preheat oven to 350°F.
- Mix two cake mixes in one large bowl according to the instructions on the packages.
- Divide the mix between 4 greased and floured stainless steel cookware: 2 rectangular cake pans; 1 round, 8"-diameter cake pan; and 1 round cake pan or stainless steel bowl 3-4" in diameter. Fill the pans and bowl about half full.
- Bake the cakes in the oven until a toothpick inserted into their centers comes out clean. The round cakes will take less time than the rectangular cakes.
- Cool on a rack. Remove cakes from cookware.
- Set the rectangular cakes side by side. Lay the round cakes on top.
- Divide icing in two separate bowls. Add green food coloring to one for the mountains and blue food coloring to the other for the ocean.
- Spread the green icing over the round cakes and the blue icing over the rectangular cakes.
- Use almond paste for the beach. Decorate with candies held in place with a dab of corn syrup.

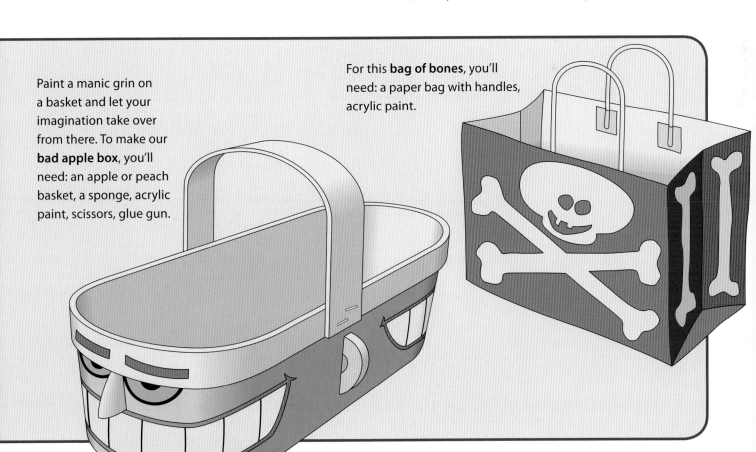

Paint a manic grin on a basket and let your imagination take over from there. To make our **bad apple box**, you'll need: an apple or peach basket, a sponge, acrylic paint, scissors, glue gun.

For this **bag of bones**, you'll need: a paper bag with handles, acrylic paint.

• To secure your design to the door, try double-sided painter's tape or florist's clay.
• Test out your choice of adhesive on a corner of the door first to avoid damaging the door surface.

Haunted House

Pull out the stops and alert the neighborhood that you're open for business—trick-or-treat style. Set a jack-o'-lantern (page 46-49) in the window, turn your yard into a cemetery (page 54), hang out some unusual spinetinglers (page 58), and put a scary dummy on guard (page 56). To create a breathtaking door, use the ideas on this page to get started and let your imagination do the rest.

Mummy Dearest

Make this menacing mummy by cutting out its shape—with or without the coffin—(pattern, page 65) from poster board. Wrap the mummy in strips of white cotton, gauze, or cheesecloth.

Fly by Night

This scene works just as well on a banner. Cut the silhouettes (patterns, page 64) from felt, then glue them to a large piece of shiny dark fabric.

Skullduggery

Cut out the skull (pattern, page 63) from poster board. Draw in the eyes, nose, and mouth with black marker or cut them out using a craft knife.

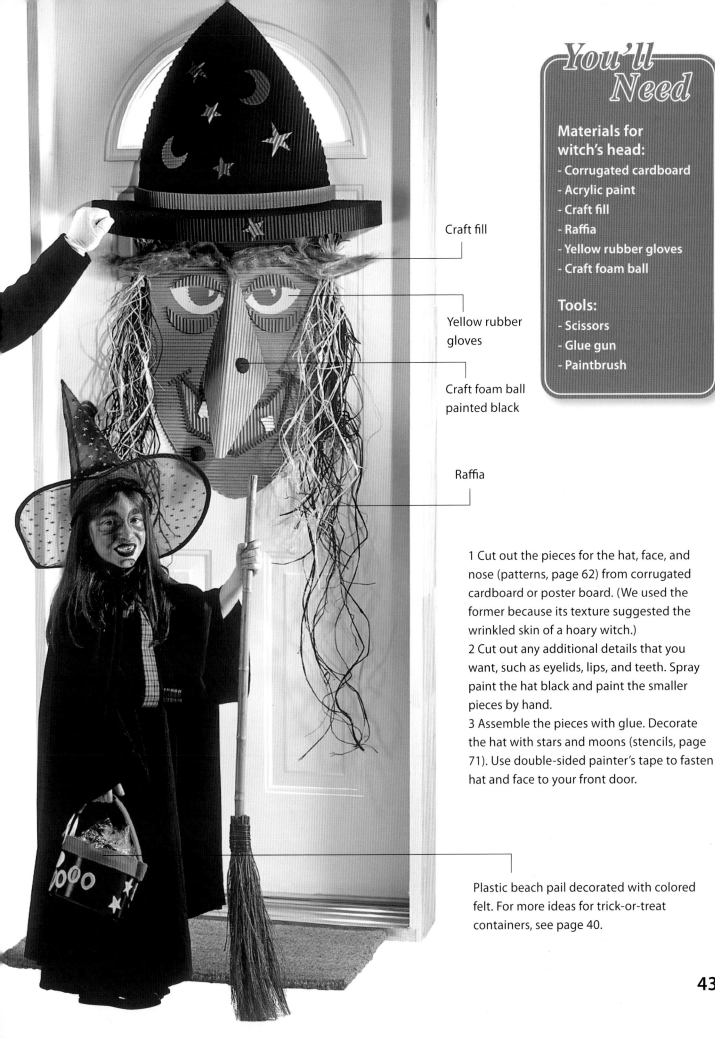

Craft fill

Yellow rubber
gloves

Craft foam ball
painted black

Raffia

1 Cut out the pieces for the hat, face, and nose (patterns, page 62) from corrugated cardboard or poster board. (We used the former because its texture suggested the wrinkled skin of a hoary witch.)
2 Cut out any additional details that you want, such as eyelids, lips, and teeth. Spray paint the hat black and paint the smaller pieces by hand.
3 Assemble the pieces with glue. Decorate the hat with stars and moons (stencils, page 71). Use double-sided painter's tape to fasten hat and face to your front door.

Plastic beach pail decorated with colored felt. For more ideas for trick-or-treat containers, see page 40.

43

Haunted House

These wild and crazy 3-D door designs delve a little further into the realm of Halloween horror. Great special effects can be created with easy-to-find household materials. With Fright Face (opposite), plastic planters are turned into big, bulging eyes; while spiralled pipe cleaners make Tombstone Tomcat's head pop-out and shake. Choose from the ideas and patterns on these pages or adapt them to bring some of your very own monsters to life!

You'll Need

Materials for Fright Face:
- Polyester lining
- Acrylic paint
- Fiber fill
- Felt
- Bristol board
- Paper plates
- Plastic planters
- Foam cord
- Styrofoam balls
- Pipe cleaners
- Steel wool

Outils:
- Scissors
- Sewing kit
- Glue gun
- Double-sided tape
- Staple gun

Tombstone Tomcat

Use two tones of deep blue felt for the background. Cut the skull, moon and clouds from colored bristol board or felt, and the cat from textured material (pattern, page 67). Mount the head on corrugated cardboard painted white, and attach it to the door surface with spiralled pipe cleaners. To make the 3-D tombstone see page 55.

Headless Jack

To create the 'misty' background, lightly spray paint a sheet of yellow bristol board with a deep purple color. Cut the body shape from two tones of felt or bristol board (pattern, page 68). For the 'head', cut a plastic jack-o'-lantern in two and glue the face side to the door. Make the hand supporting the head in a similar way to the one on page 55. Glue or tape it in position.

Drawbridge

The bricks, eyes, and other shapes that make up this castle entrance are cut from colored bristol board or felt and glued to a brown bristol board background (pattern, page 69). With a marker, add lines to a sheet of corrugated cardboard for the drawbridge. Fasten two lengths of large metal-colored plastic chain to the door frame and bridge with silver duct tape. For added effect, add a plastic spider and artificial spider web.

44

1 Measure and cut a piece of black felt for the door and fasten it with double-sided tape.

2 Cut the mouth and teeth shapes from the pink felt and white bristol board (pattern, page 66), and glue to the black felt.

3 To make the eyes, glue red pipe-cleaners to the sides of the white plastic planters. Paint the paper plates and glue them to the planter bottoms, then line the seams with flexible foam cord. Next, skewer styrofoam balls with spiralled pipe-cleaners and staple the ends to the plates. Fasten the completed eye assemblies to the door by gluing along the planter edges.

4 Shape the eyebrows from steel wool and glue or staple them above the eye assemblies.

5 For the lips and tongue, cut out two pieces of red lining material to the size shown in the pattern. Sew the edges of the shapes, leaving one end open, then loosely stuff them with fibre fill. Sew the openings shut, and add a center line of stitching to the tongue. Glue or staple the lips and tongue in place.

Black felt

Steel wool

Pipe cleaners

Paper plates, painted blue

Plastic planters

Bristol board

Pink felt

Polyester liner

Pumpkin Panache

It's hard to imagine Halloween without at least one pumpkin on display. Whether you decide to cut a jack-o'-lantern or decorate without carving (page 48), keep in mind that the shape of the pumpkin is as much a part of its final expression as its eyes, ears, nose, or mouth.

Cleaning out the interior of a pumpkin is a messy job. Be sure to protect your work area with cardboard or newspaper.

1 Carve a circle around the stem and remove the lid. Scoop out the pumpkin flesh with a long-handled spoon. Sketch a face on the pumpkin or, if using one of our cutouts (pages 78-79), tape it to the pumpkin. Punch holes into the pumpkin every 1/2 inch or so along the lines.

2 If you used a cutout, remove it before deepening the puncture holes. The holes make the carving a lot easier.

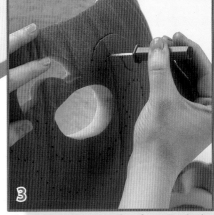

3 Carve out the pumpkin face. Push the pieces through to get them out. Put a candle inside and set the pumpkin in a safe place before you light it. Alternatively light it with a flashlight.

47

Pumpkin Panache

Here's a pretty patch of pumpkins to inspire your creative efforts. Rummage through your home—your vegetable crisper, jewelry box, toolbox, and sewing kit—for ordinary items that you can put to use.

Peghead Pete
We painted his cartoon face and clothespin locks with acrylic paint.

Wacky Wendy
We raided the bathroom for her hair curlers, the kitchen for her mouth, the sewing kit for her nose and her eyeballs, and the toy shelf for her ears.

Sink strainer and button

Pasta

Cosmetic sponge

Sink plug

Zipper

Swimming goggles

Grinning Gertie
This pumpkin's button-eyed, but her smile is genuine marble.

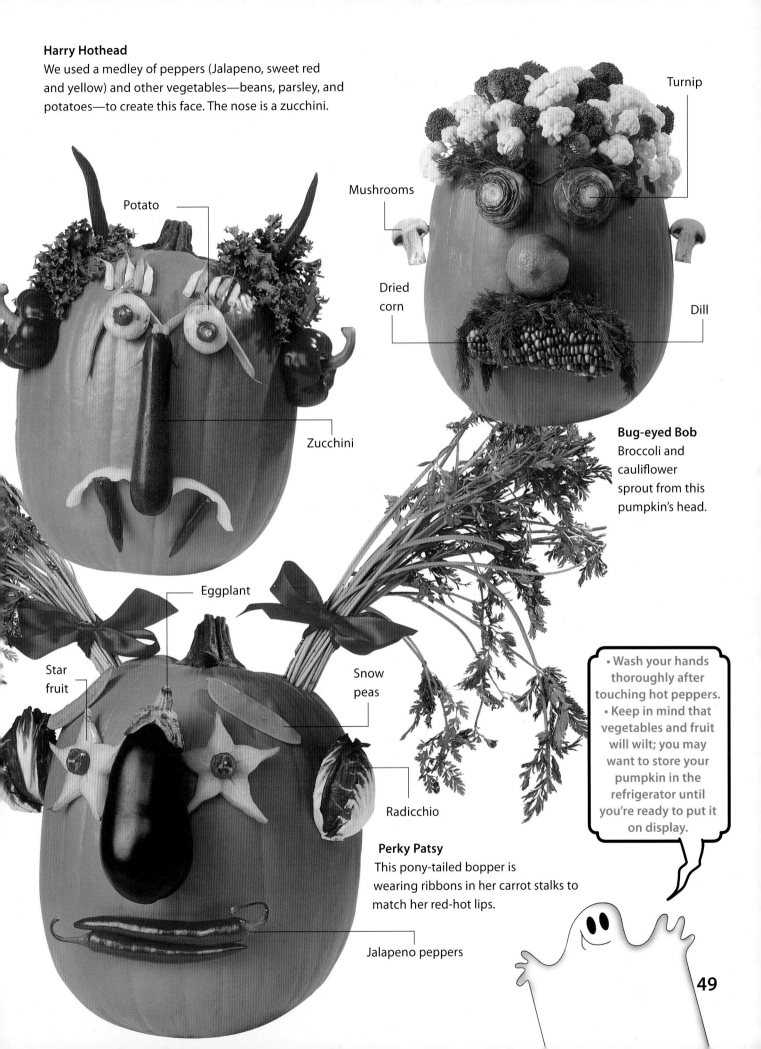

Harry Hothead
We used a medley of peppers (Jalapeno, sweet red and yellow) and other vegetables—beans, parsley, and potatoes—to create this face. The nose is a zucchini.

Potato

Zucchini

Turnip

Mushrooms

Dried corn

Dill

Bug-eyed Bob
Broccoli and cauliflower sprout from this pumpkin's head.

Eggplant

Star fruit

Snow peas

Radicchio

Perky Patsy
This pony-tailed bopper is wearing ribbons in her carrot stalks to match her red-hot lips.

Jalapeno peppers

- Wash your hands thoroughly after touching hot peppers.
- Keep in mind that vegetables and fruit will wilt; you may want to store your pumpkin in the refrigerator until you're ready to put it on display.

49

The History of Halloween

The origins of Halloween date back to the 5th century B.C. to Celtic Ireland. The Celts considered October 31st the start of the New Year, and they believed that on this night wandering spirits of the dead would return to earth to walk among the living In the 8th century, the Pope declared November 1st to be All Saints Day, also called All Hallows Day, which is where our word "Halloween" comes from.

According to folklore, the Celts used to disguise themselves in scary costumes, as witches, warlocks and goblins, in order to frighten the visiting spirits away This is where our tradition of dressing up on Halloween comes from.

It is said that the Celts used to ward off the visiting spirits by making their homes as dark, damp and unviting as possible.

Why are pumpkins such a big part of Halloween?

According to the legend of the "Jack-o'-Lantern," there was once a trickster named Jack who angered both God and the Devil, and was destined to walk the earth forever, with only one ember to light his way. The Irish commemorated this mythical ghost by putting embers in hollowed-out turnips, which they left on their front steps. In the 1850s, Irish immigrants brought this custom to the U.S., where they found a plentiful supply of pumpkins. They have been part of our Halloween ever since.

Feathers and contruction paper create the head and wings for this Halloween rooster, while natural bumps and creases make up grandma Halloween's face.

Pumpkins and gourds of different sizes work in combination with dried foliage to create this winsome foul (below).

The possibilities are as limitless as your imagination. Dried flowers make up Philomene's hair (above), while cardboard and papier mâché put the finishing touches to this extra-large burger (left).

Garden of Horrors

Create a frightfully spooky welcome for your trick-or-treating neighbors by turning your front garden into a temporary graveyard. All Hallows' Eve was once believed to be the night when the souls of the dead arose from their graves to wander the world.

So include some props in your cemetery—a stuffed glove perhaps, or a pair of old shoes—to suggest that your corpse is set to roam!

R.I.P.
Headless Hank
1813-1885

I shall return...

The bat and the raven (patterns, page 71) were cut out of black foamcore. The bat flies above the tombstone on the end of a piece of wire glued to the back of the tombstone.

We cut a discarded pair of rubber-soled shoes in half and planted the toes in the dirt.

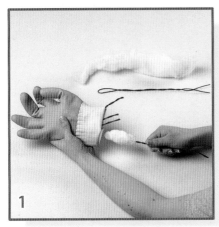

1

For the hand, cut five pieces of 16 gauge wire, each about 2' long. Bend each wire in half and twist it. Wrap craft fill around the folded ends and stick them into the glove fingers. Stuff the rest of the glove with craft fill.

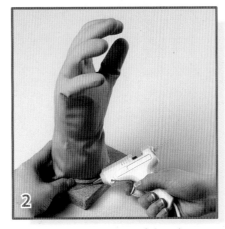

2

Glue the bottom part of the glove to a piece of wood. Plant the wood base in the burial site. We wrapped gauze around the base of the hand to simulate lacey cuffs.

You'll Need

Materials for the hand:
- Yellow rubber glove
- 16 gauge wire
- Craft fill
- Wood for stand
- Gauze

Tools for the hand:
- Wire cutters
- Pliers
- Glue gun

Materials for the headstone:
- Polystyrene
- Gray spray paint
- Black acrylic paint

Tools for the headstone:
- Craft knife
- Sandpaper
- Paintbrush

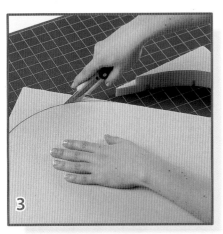

3

For the headstone, outline its shape on a large sheet of polystyrene and cut it out with a craft knife. (We used a sheet 2'x2'x2".) Smooth rough edges with sandpaper.

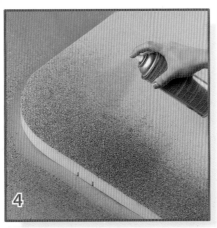

4

Spray paint the headstone gray. (Our craft store carries a spray paint that resembles granite, which is even better).

5

Paint the "deceased's" name, dates, and perhaps a brief epitaph on the headstone in black acrylic paint. (You can buy a stencil of the alphabet and numerals and use that if you prefer.)

Porch Spook

A porch spook is easy and inexpensive to make. Begin with the head, either making it as we've shown here or stuffing a white T-shirt, then tying off both ends with string. Make the body by filling old clothes with newspaper or rags. Dress a hillbilly in denim overalls, a checkered shirt, and a pair of rubber boots. Adorn a scarecrow with a corncob pipe and add lots of straw. Dr. Frankenstein's monster (right) is wearing a shabby black suit.

You'll Need

Materials:
-White cotton
-Craft fill
-2 cardboard tubes
-String or wire
-Old clothes
-Rubber gloves
-Boots
-Acrylic paint
-Synthetic fur

Tools:
-Scissors
-Glue gun
-Paintbrush
-Markers

We used black marker to paint nails on rubber gloves.

The telltale screw was made of different sized rolls of corrugated cardboard, glued together and spray painted metallic silver.

To make the head, make a cross with two rectangular pieces of white cotton. (Our pieces were 9"x 40" each.) Glue the sides together to make a box.

Stuff the head and insert a pole about 2' long. (Cardboard tubes used for Christmas wrapping work well.) Secure the neck with string.

• Instead of painting on the face, you can use buttons, cork, stones, marbles, string, shells, etc.

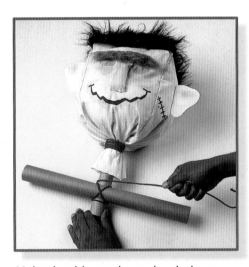

Make a nose and ears with scraps of fabric. We stuffed this nose with craft fill to get an imposing shape. Draw on a face with markers and use more craft fill for the eyebrows and synthetic fur for the hair.

Make shoulders to hang the clothes on by tying a second pole or tube crosswise to the first. Create the body with clothes of your choice, stuffing them with rags or newspaper as you go.

Ghostly Teasers

We cut the phantom from white foamcore and drew its face with black marker.

Strange sounds and sights create a haunting atmosphere. Make a mobile that rustles or clangs in the wind and prop up a silhouette in your window. Check out the patterns (page 71) for one that you like or use the phantom (page 61) as we did here. Make it large enough to fill the window and set a light behind it.

58

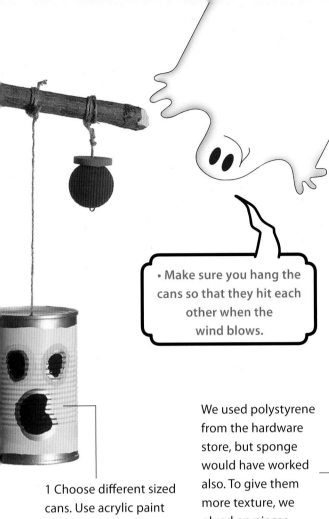

The witch's hats are miniature versions of the one we made on page 14. Instead of a cardboard brim however, we used black rubber rings from the craft store.

• Make sure you hang the cans so that they hit each other when the wind blows.

We used polystyrene from the hardware store, but sponge would have worked also. To give them more texture, we glued on pieces of twine and then painted over them in orange. The stems (pattern, page 67) are cut from green foam sheets.

Cats (pattern, page 71)

1 Choose different sized cans. Use acrylic paint to create your designs.

2 Punch a hole in the bottom of the cans with a hammer and nail. Thread string through the hole and knot it so it doesn't slip out. Then hang the cans on different lengths of string from a branch.

3 We used foam balls and rings from the craftstore for the extra decorations. To hang, thread a 2" piece of wire through the ball and ring, loop the ends with pliers, and tie with twine.

You'll Need

Materials for Tin Can Mobile:
- Cans (at least 3 of different sizes)
- Acrylic paint
- Twine
- Tree branch
- Foam balls and rings
- Wire (18 gauge)

Tools:
- Paintbrush
- Hammer
- Nail
- Pliers

Materials for Cat Mobile:
- Wreath
- Twine
- For hats, poster board, ribbon, black rubber rings
- For pumpkins, 1"-thick polystyrene sheet, green foam sheets
- For cats, poster board

Tools:
- Craft knife
- Scissors
- Paintbrush

59

Patterns & Cutouts

Here are the patterns and cutouts to help you complete some of the costumes and props in this book. We used a grid of 1/2" squares for our patterns and for each one we have provided the figure you need to enlarge it to the size we used. Use a photocopier or the grid method to ensure that the enlarged pattern is proportionate. Once you have determined the size you want (eg. graph paper with 1" squares for a 200% enlargement, or graph paper with 2" squares for a 400% enlargement), copy the pattern, square by square, onto your graph paper, following the same angles and curves. Tape the enlarged pattern to the surface of the material you plan to use and cut around it with scissors or a craft knife.

• To make really gigantic patterns (such as those on page 61) photocopy the pattern as large as you can. Cut it out. Hang an enormous piece of white paper (such as pattern paper available in fabric stores) on the wall. In a darkened room hold the pattern between a lit lamp and the wall, while a helper outlines the silhouette on the paper. Remove the paper from the wall and cut out the enlarged pattern.

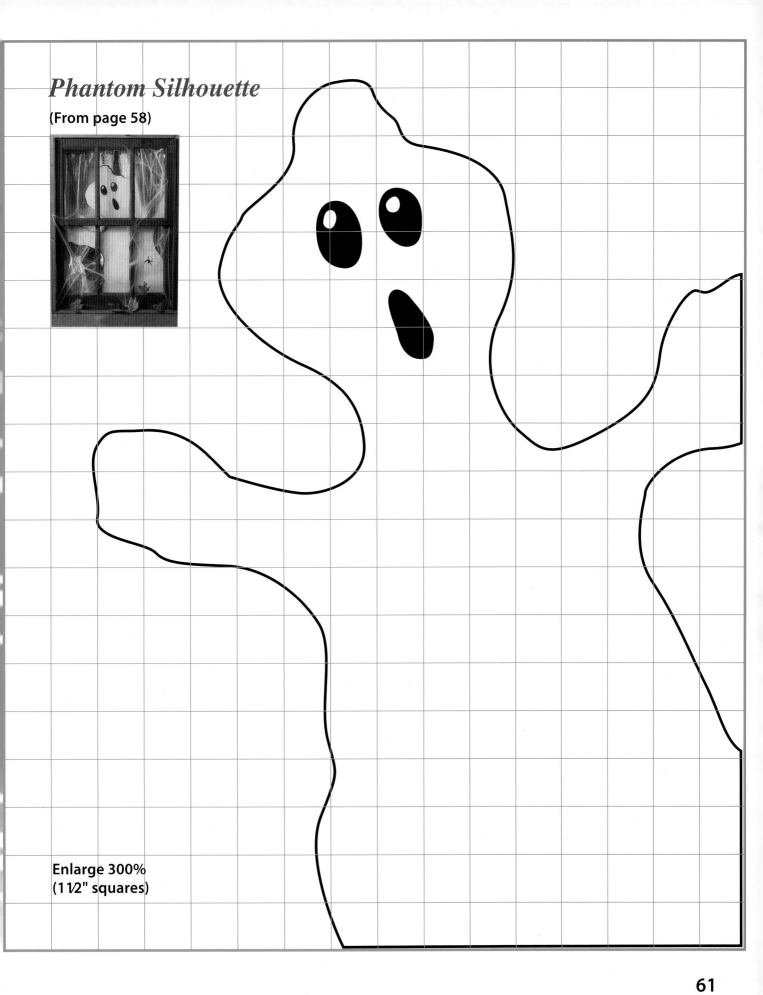

Phantom Silhouette

(From page 58)

Enlarge 300%
(1 1/2" squares)

61

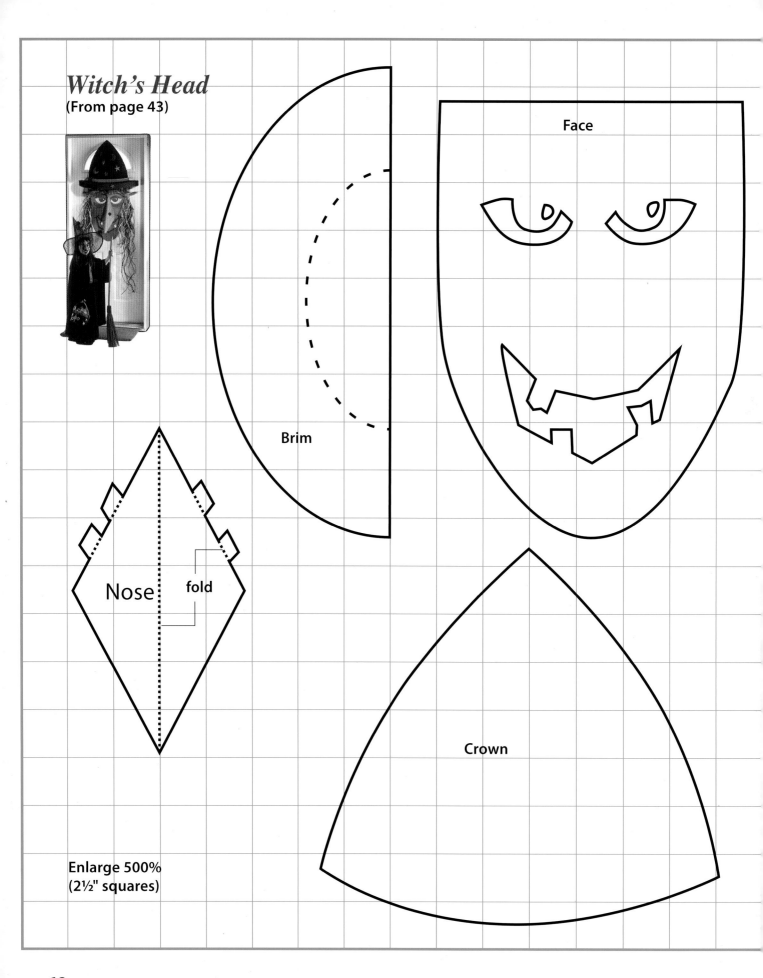

Witch's Head
(From page 43)

Face

Brim

Nose

fold

Crown

Enlarge 500%
(2½" squares)

Skullduggery
(From page 42)

Enlarge 800%
(4" squares)

Fly By Night
(From page 42)

Enlarge 750%
(3 ¾" squares)

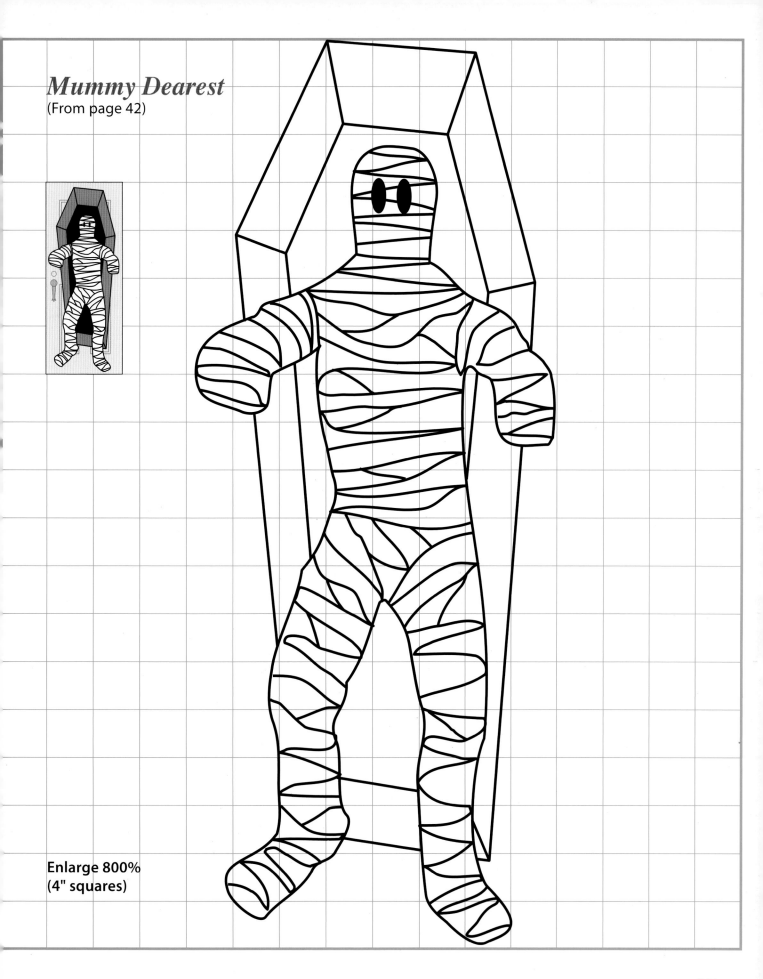

Mummy Dearest
(From page 42)

Enlarge 800%
(4" squares)

Fright Face
(From page 45)

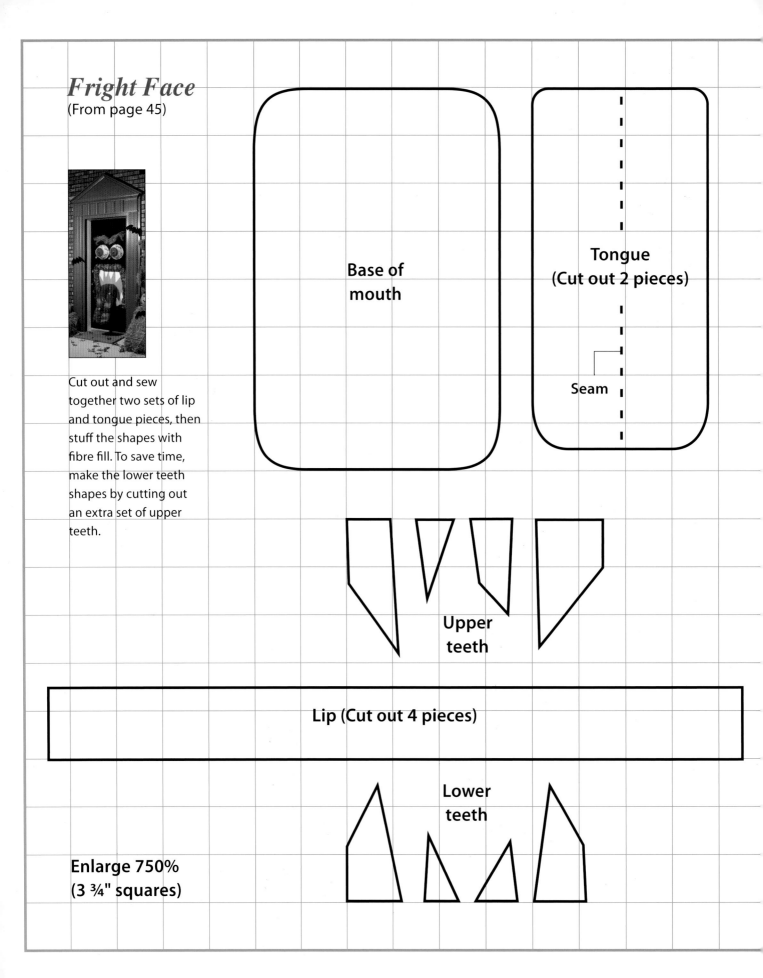

Cut out and sew together two sets of lip and tongue pieces, then stuff the shapes with fibre fill. To save time, make the lower teeth shapes by cutting out an extra set of upper teeth.

Base of mouth

Tongue (Cut out 2 pieces)

Seam

Upper teeth

Lip (Cut out 4 pieces)

Lower teeth

Enlarge 750% (3 ¾" squares)

Tombstone
Tomcat
(From page 44)

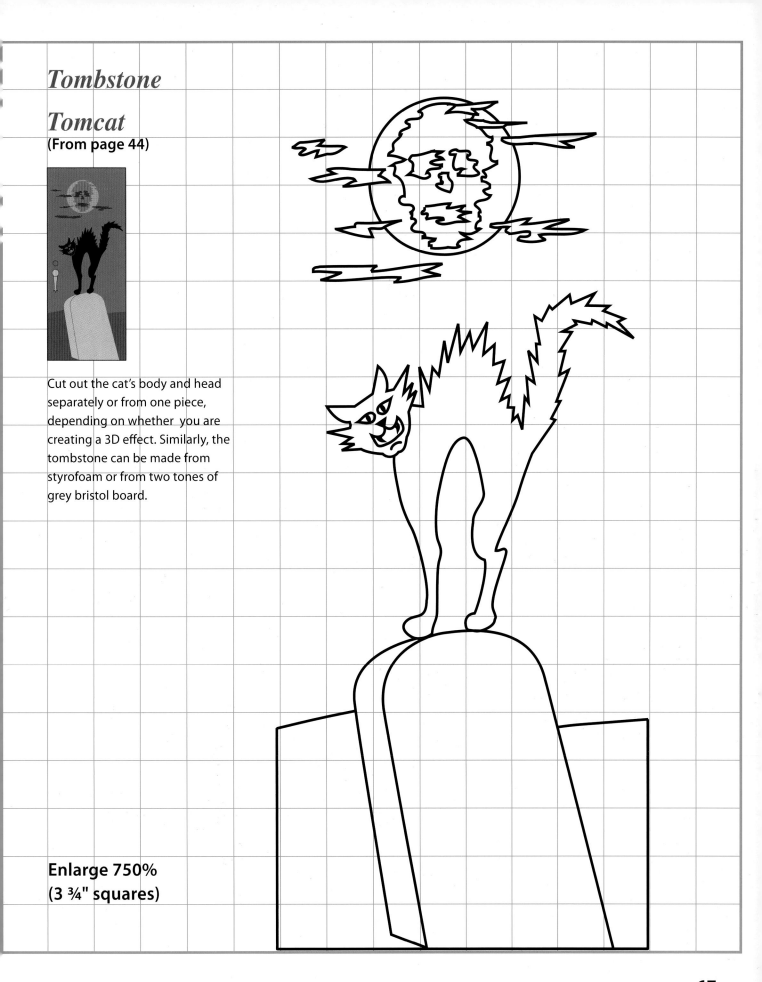

Cut out the cat's body and head separately or from one piece, depending on whether you are creating a 3D effect. Similarly, the tombstone can be made from styrofoam or from two tones of grey bristol board.

**Enlarge 750%
(3 ¾" squares)**

Headless Jack

(From page 44)

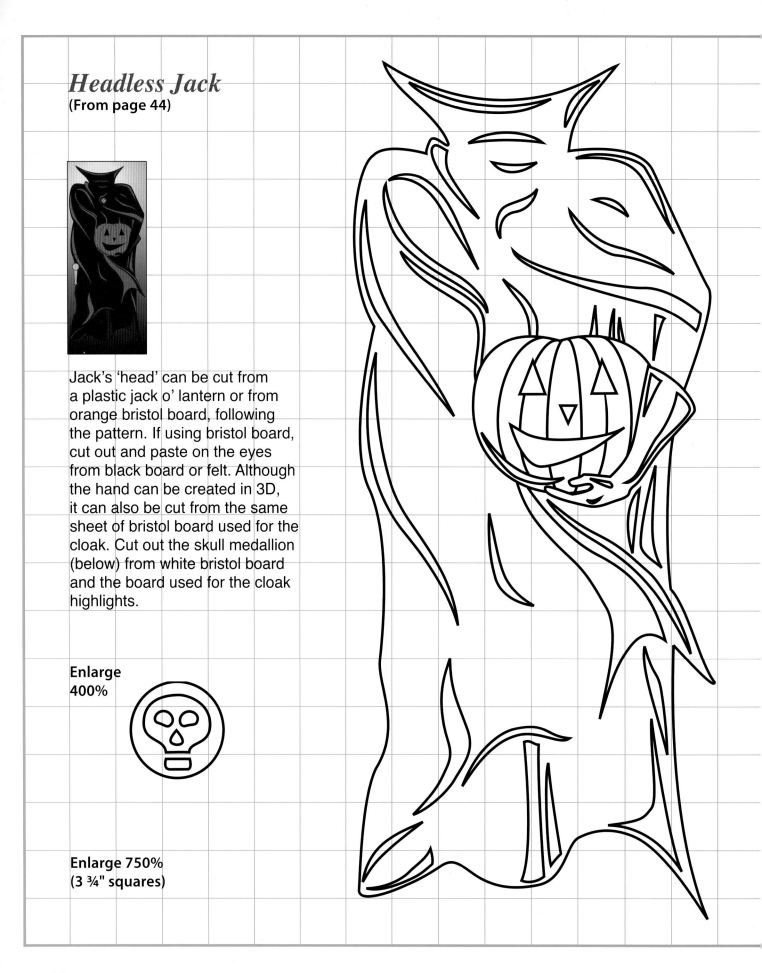

Jack's 'head' can be cut from
a plastic jack o' lantern or from
orange bristol board, following
the pattern. If using bristol board,
cut out and paste on the eyes
from black board or felt. Although
the hand can be created in 3D,
it can also be cut from the same
sheet of bristol board used for the
cloak. Cut out the skull medallion
(below) from white bristol board
and the board used for the cloak
highlights.

**Enlarge
400%**

**Enlarge 750%
(3 ¾" squares)**

Drawbridge

(From page 44)

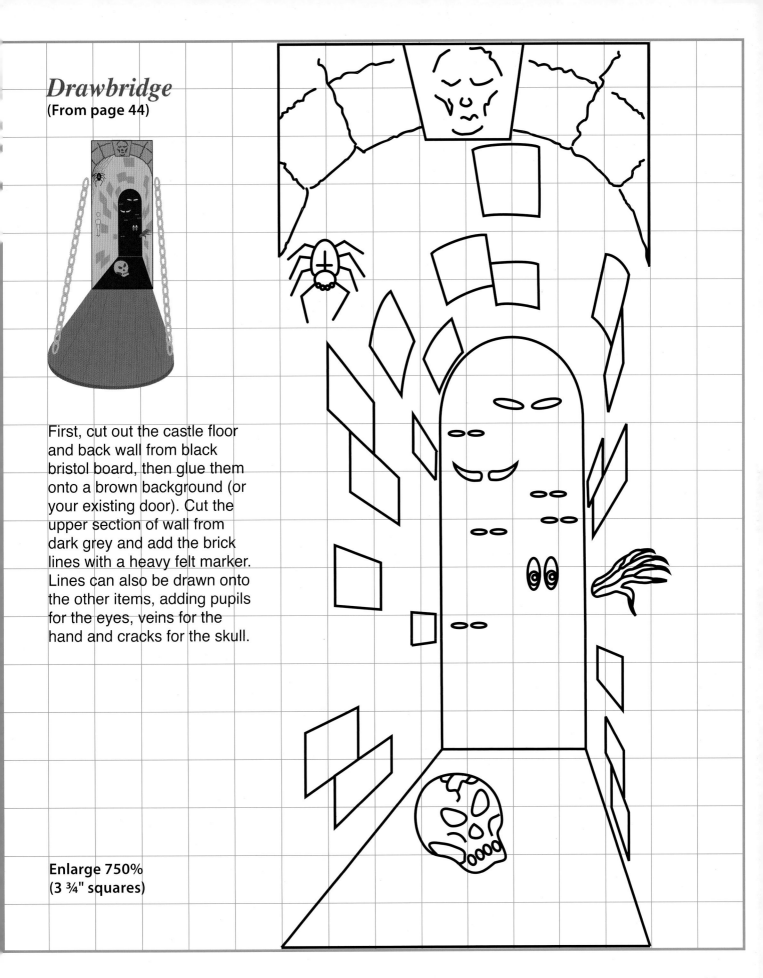

First, cut out the castle floor and back wall from black bristol board, then glue them onto a brown background (or your existing door). Cut the upper section of wall from dark grey and add the brick lines with a heavy felt marker. Lines can also be drawn onto the other items, adding pupils for the eyes, veins for the hand and cracks for the skull.

Enlarge 750%
(3 ¾" squares)

69

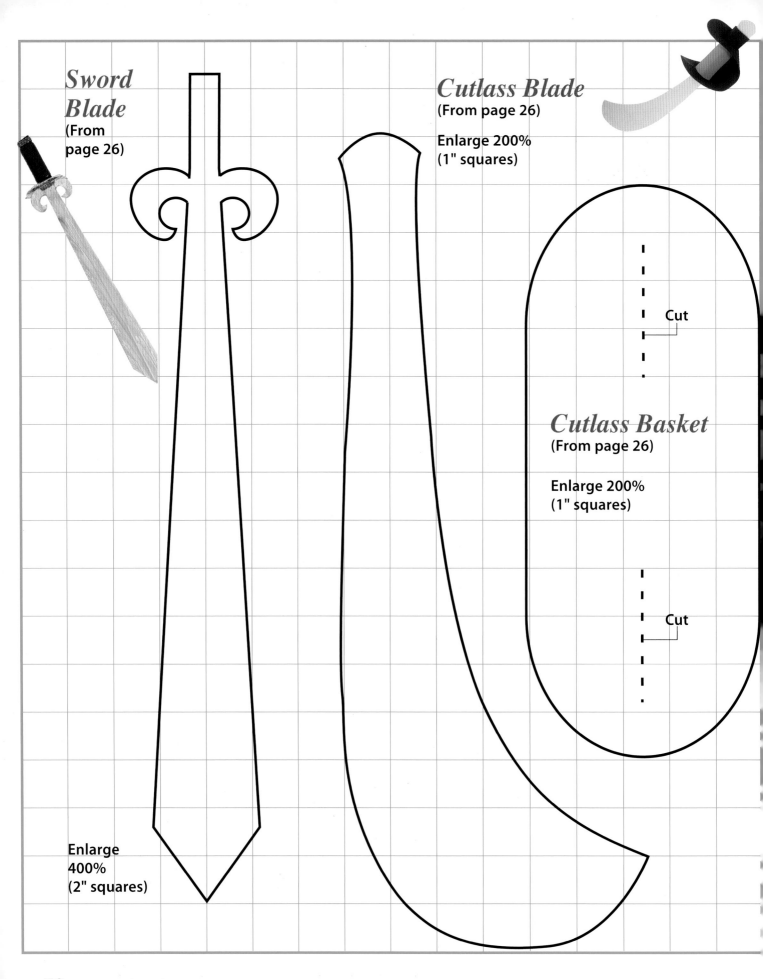

Sword Blade

(From page 26)

Cutlass Blade

(From page 26)

Enlarge 200%
(1" squares)

Cut

Cutlass Basket

(From page 26)

Enlarge 200%
(1" squares)

Cut

Enlarge
400%
(2" squares)

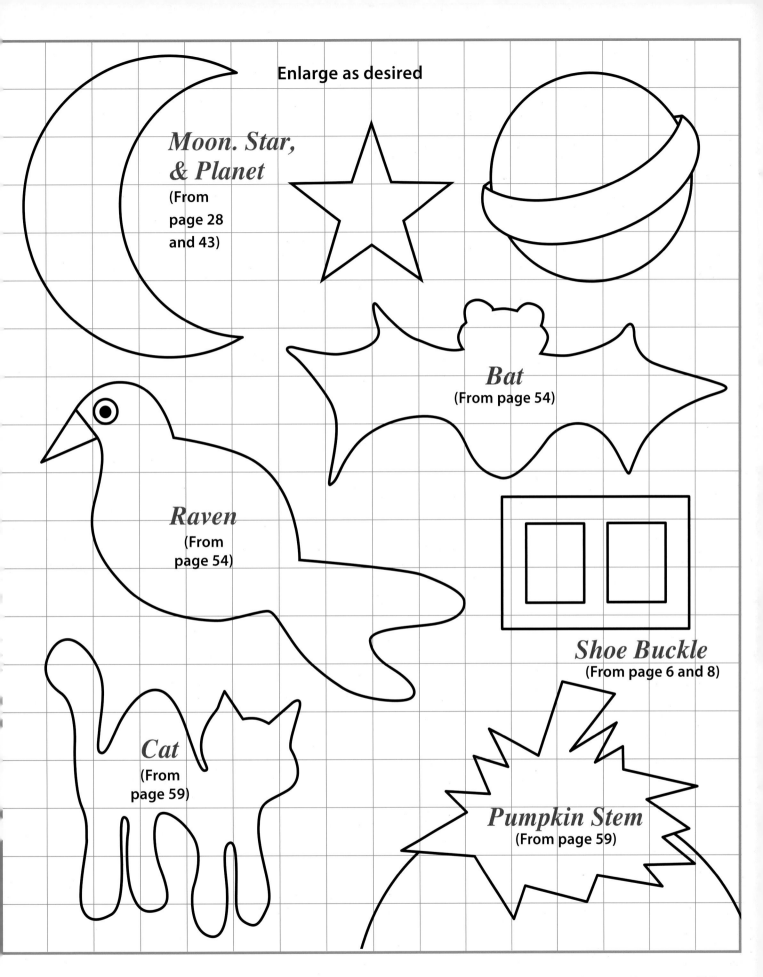

Enlarge as desired

*Moon. Star,
& Planet*
(From
page 28
and 43)

Bat
(From page 54)

Raven
(From
page 54)

Shoe Buckle
(From page 6 and 8)

Cat
(From
page 59)

Pumpkin Stem
(From page 59)

Robin Hood's Cap
(From page 15)

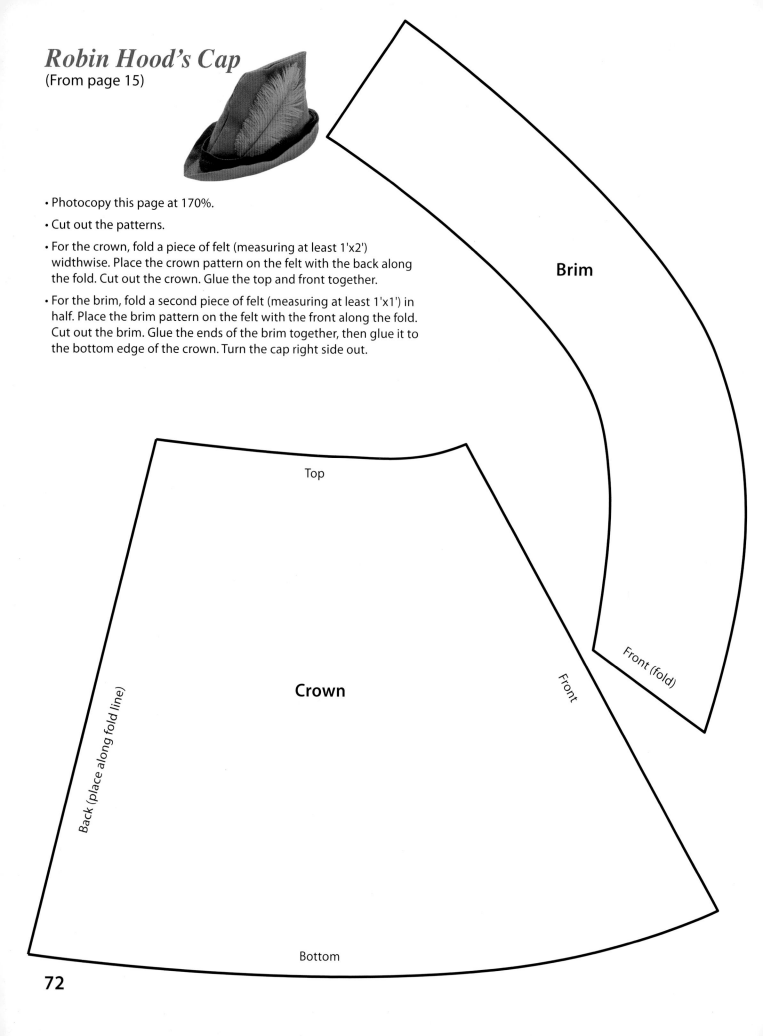

- Photocopy this page at 170%.

- Cut out the patterns.

- For the crown, fold a piece of felt (measuring at least 1'x2') widthwise. Place the crown pattern on the felt with the back along the fold. Cut out the crown. Glue the top and front together.

- For the brim, fold a second piece of felt (measuring at least 1'x1') in half. Place the brim pattern on the felt with the front along the fold. Cut out the brim. Glue the ends of the brim together, then glue it to the bottom edge of the crown. Turn the cap right side out.

Brim

Top

Front (fold)

Front

Crown

Back (place along fold line)

Bottom

Lion's Hood

(From page 22)

- Make a photocopy of this page.
- Cut out the patterns.
- Make 2 photocopies of the side flap at 180%.
- Make 4 photocopies of the ear at 180%.
- Cut the crown piece in half. Photocopy each half at 180%. Tape the halves together.
- Cut fabric, using the patterns.
- Glue the side flaps to the crown, making a hood.
- Make the ears and glue them to the top of the hood.

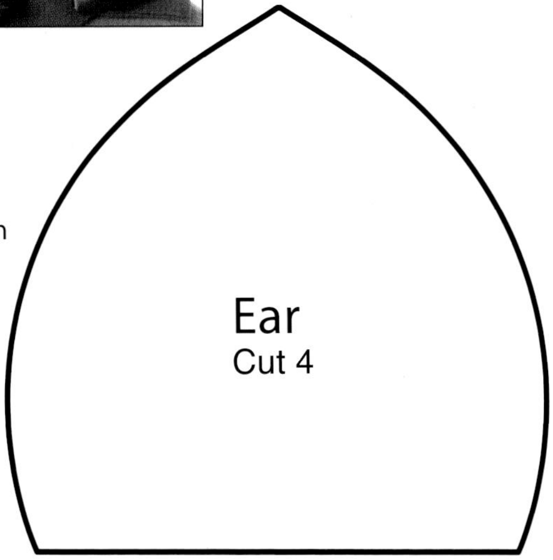

Ear
Cut 4

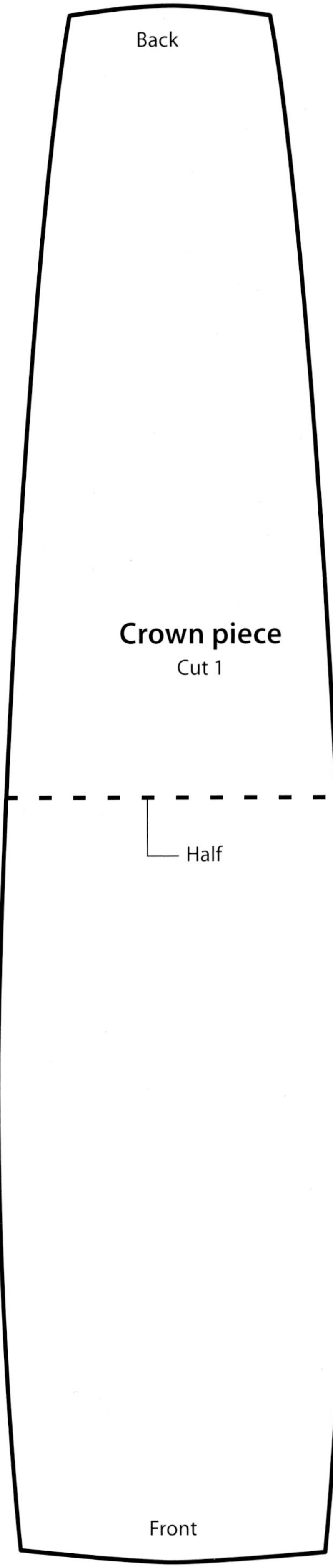

Side flap
Cut 2

Back

Crown piece
Cut 1

Half

Front

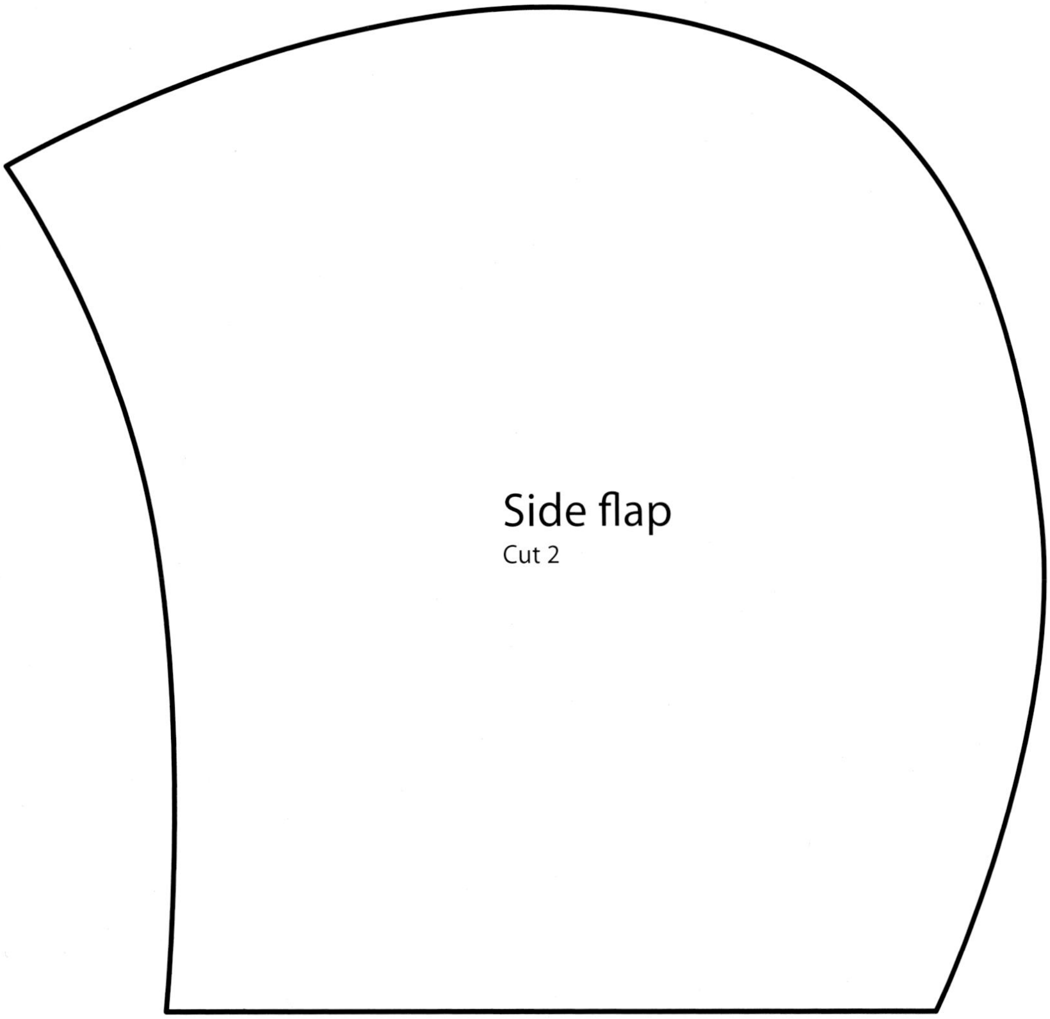

73

Mask Parade
(From page 16)

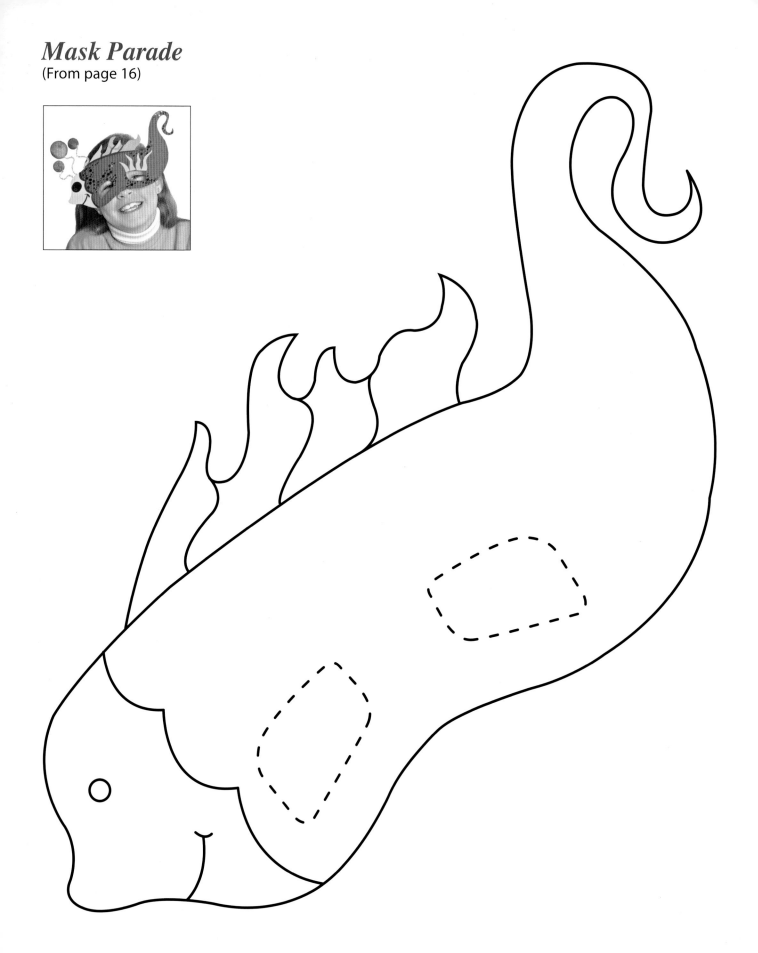

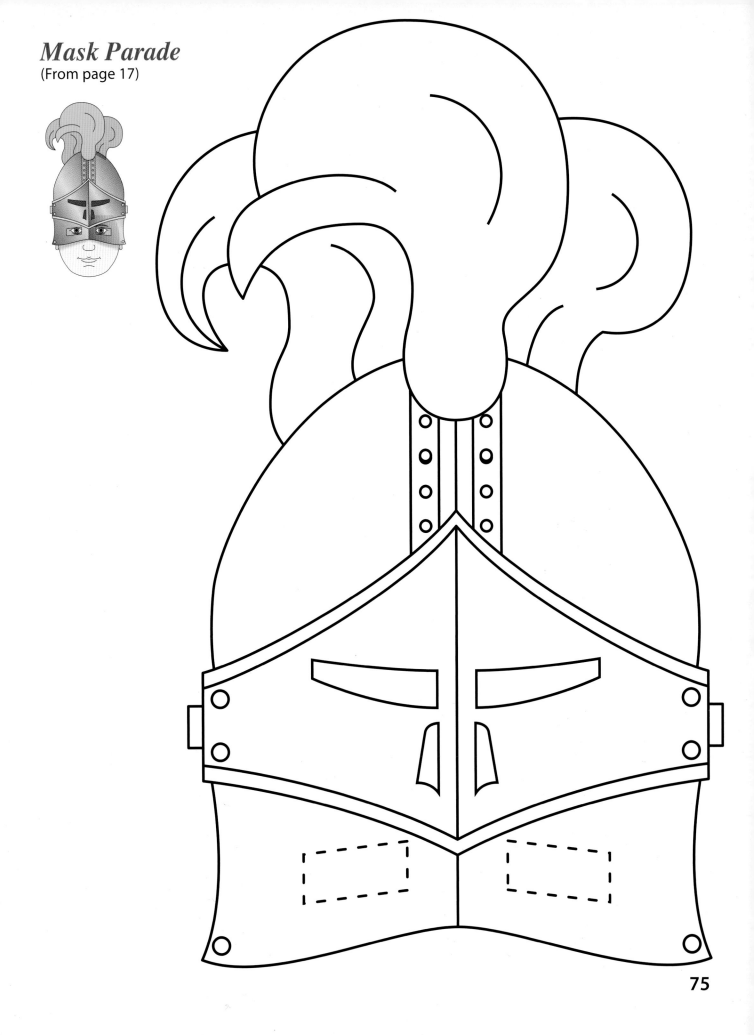

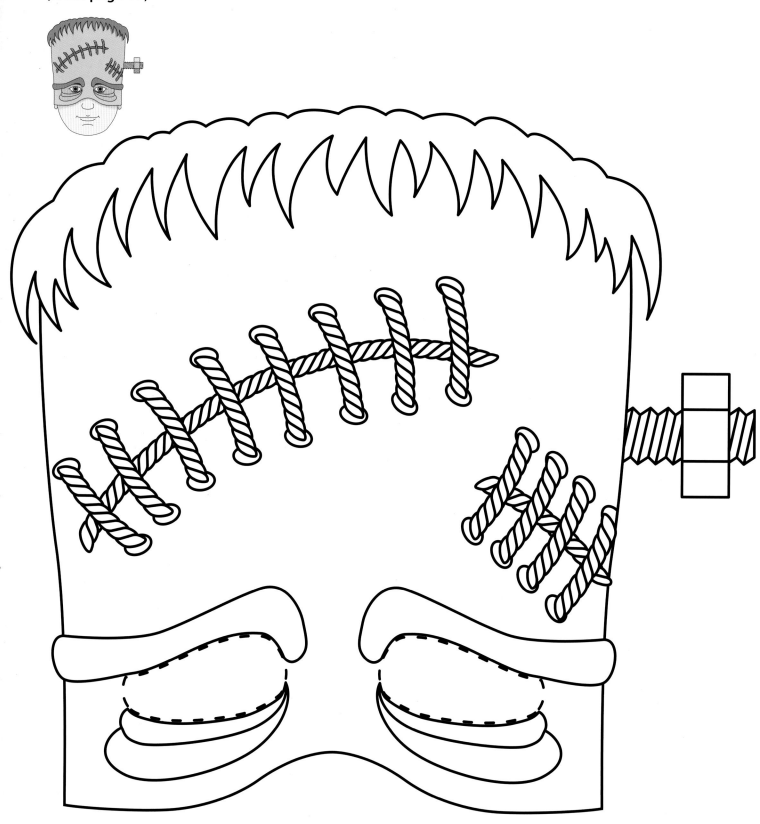

Pumpkin Panache
(From page 46)

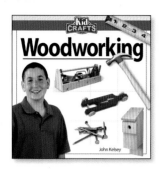

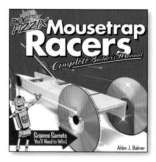
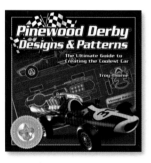